1111 AMAZING FACTS ABOUT
ANIMALS

Jack Goldstein

Published in 2015 by
AUK Authors, an imprint of
Andrews UK Limited
www.andrewsuk.com

Copyright © 2015 Jack Goldstein

The right of Jack Goldstein to be identified as the author of this work has been asserted in accordance with the Copyright, Designs and Patents Act 1988

All rights reserved. No part of this publication may be reproduced, stored in or introduced into a retrieval system, or transmitted, in any form, or by any means (electronic, mechanical, photocopying, recording or otherwise) without the prior written permission of the publisher. Any person who does any unauthorised act in relation to this publication may be liable to criminal prosecution and civil claims for damages.

All facts contained within this book have been researched from reputable sources. If any information is found to be false, please contact the publishers, who will be happy to make corrections for future editions.

Photograph Credits

Thorny devil photograph courtesy of Jarrod – lostandcold
Brookesia micra photograph courtesy of Frank Glaw, Jörn Köhler, Ted M Townsend and Miguel Vences
Frill necked lizard photograph courtesy of Matt Clancy
Panther chameleon photograph courtesy of fRandi-Shooters
Horned Viper photograph courtesy of H Krisp
Timber rattlesnake photograph courtesy of Tad Arensmeier
Indian cobra photograph courtesy of Kevin Jones
Boa constrictor photograph courtesy of Christian Mehlführer
Anaconda photograph courtesy of Dave Lovesdale.

Contents

101 Amazing Facts about Dinosaurs	1
101 Amazing Facts about Dogs	29
101 Amazing Facts about Lizards	53
101 Amazing Facts about Insects	77
101 Amazing Facts about Sharks	99
101 Amazing Facts about Cats	121
101 Amazing Facts about Birds	139
101 Amazing Facts about Horses	159
101 Amazing Facts about Snakes	181
101 Amazing Facts about Spiders	203
101 Amazing Facts about Fish	227

Introduction

Did you know that in medieval times dogs were known to have accompanied their masters into battle wearing suits of armour? Or that cows from different regions moo in different accents? Were you aware that the courtship dance of some seahorses can last eight hours? Or that an albatross flies much further in a lifetime than the Apollo astronauts did on their moon missions? This fantastic book contains over one thousand facts about a wide range of animals, including dinosaurs, dogs, lizards, insects, sharks, cats, birds, horses, snakes, spiders and fish. So if you want to know what the wagometer was invented for, which fish the Romans used as a recreational drug or what the offspring of a donkey and a zebra is called, then this is the book for you!

THE FACTS

101 Amazing Facts about Dinosaurs

THE BASICS

- The word *dinosaur* was invented in 1842 by a British palaeontologist called Robert Owen. It means 'terrible lizard' when translated from the Greek words *deinos* and *sauros*.

- When talking about dinosaurs, one is most commonly referring to reptiles that lived on the earth between 231.4 million and 66 million years ago.

- To put this into perspective, humans have lived on the earth for around two million years, whereas dinosaurs roamed for more than eighty times that!

- This period is known as the *Mesozoic* era, which means 'middle life' (referring to the age of the earth itself). It is further split into three periods: *Triassic* (231.4–201 million years ago), *Jurassic* (201–145 million years ago) and *Cretaceous* (145–66 million years ago).

- The first dinosaurs were quite small, however larger species evolved through the Jurassic and Cretaceous periods.

- Dinosaurs lived on all continents of the earth – even Antarctica. During the early Mesozoic era however, the earth looked very different as all of the continents were in fact one big land mass which we now call *Pangaea*. It started to break up around 200 million years ago, and the continents we know today have been drifting apart ever since.

- We still do not know how many species of dinosaur there were, with estimates ranging from one to three thousand non-avian species alone.

- 66 million years ago, there was a mass extinction of dinosaurs and other animals which is known as the *Cretaceous-Tertiary Extinction Event*.

- Scientists believe that dinosaurs included both cold-blooded and warm-blooded species, with the larger plant-eaters almost certainly being cold-blooded and the fast, active meat-eaters warm.

- We do not know for sure is what caused the mass extinction. One popular theory amongst scientists is that a huge meteorite six miles in diameter hit Mexico that would have sent shockwaves throughout the earth, wiping out everything but the smallest species of animal. We have discovered a 112-mile wide crater that *supports* this theory, although it does not *prove* it. Another theory suggests an increase in the number of animals using dinosaur eggs as a food source, leading to dwindling numbers; yet another is a plague that quickly spread across the globe.

General Facts – Part 1

- Although this book does include facts and information about them, species such as the pterodactyl are *technically* flying reptiles and *not* dinosaurs; similarly plesiosaurs and the like are water-based reptiles. It is therefore more correct to call these other species *prehistoric creatures*.

- Someone who studies dinosaurs (and other prehistoric creatures) is known as a *palaeontologist*.

- Many dinosaurs, particularly herbivores, lived in herds for protection just as some species do today. These herds could range in size from just a few animals to thousands of individuals.

- The best fossils tend to come from dinosaurs that lived near water – it is thought that the soft, muddy ground has helped preserve them better than those in other dryer areas.

- Birds are the closest living relatives of dinosaurs. Next time you see a chicken, look at it very closely – you might be surprised as to just how ancient it seems!

- In fact, chickens are so closely related to the prehistoric beasts that scientist are trying to create dinosaurs by manipulating the DNA of normal chickens! Amazingly, they believe that only a few small alterations are required.

- In 1824, William Buckland became the first person to identify dinosaur bones correctly, naming a fossil *megalosaurus*.

- Recognition should also be given to Gideon Mantell, who discovered dinosaur teeth and bones in Sussex in 1822. However, other pioneering scientists – including William Buckland – dismissed his findings as being those of fish and other animals rather than dinosaurs!
- The first dinosaur discovery in North America was in 1854 when Ferdinand Vandiveer Hayden explored the upper Missouri river and found a collection of teeth. These were later found to have belonged to trachodon, troodon and deinodon.
- Each dinosaur had its own defense mechanism. Some, obviously, had very sharp teeth and claws; others had horns or spikes, and stegosaurus had bony plates on its back – although there is some debate as to whether these were actually used as a weapon.

Unusual Dinosaurs

- There was a prehistoric creature which lived during the Cretaceous period called *deinosuchus*. It was very closely related to today's alligators – although it was around eight times as big.

- *Corythosaurus* had a large bony crest on top of its head, containing a large hollow chamber into which its nasal passages extended. This acted as an amplifier for sound, and it is thought that it could have had a cry much like the sound of a trumpet.

- The skull of the *pentaceratops* (a dinosaur with five horns on its head) was an amazing three metres long.

- The *quetzalcoatlus*, a pterosaur from the late cretaceous period, had a wingspan of at least eleven metres – and some think it could have been as much as twenty! This makes it one of the largest flying creatures the earth has ever seen.

- *Therizinosaurus* had claws which were each a whole metre long. Scary!

- It is thought that the *troodon* was the most intelligent of all the dinosaurs. It lived around 77 million years ago, was around two metres long and had the brain the size of a comparable mammal today.

- *Therizinosaurus* had extremely long and thin claws, effectively like medieval swords. With three on each hand, this was certainly a dinosaur you wouldn't want to mess with.

- *Archelon* was a sea turtle that lived around eighty million years ago, measuring four metres long and almost five metres wide from flipper to flipper.
- *Sinornithosaurus* was a small, turkey-sized member of the raptor family that had long fang-like teeth that scientists believe were used to inject venom into its prey.
- *Oryctodromeus cubicularis* burrowed under the ground with its shovel-like snout; its name literally means 'digging runner of the lair'.

Records

- The earliest dinosaur that we have discovered has been named *eoraptor*, meaning 'dawn stealer', as it lived at the dawn of the era of dinosaurs. It was around two feet long and weighed five pounds, with sharp teeth and claws.

- The *stegosaurus* had the smallest brain in comparison to its body size; whereas its body was as large as a family car, its brain was only the size of a walnut!

- Although we think of dinosaurs as huge, the blue whale is the largest creature to have ever lived on the earth, and is in fact twice as long as the biggest aquatic dinosaur, *liopluerodon*.

- The smallest dinosaur discovered so far is the *microraptor*, which was found in China and measures just 40cm in length. A smaller dinosaur called *mussaurus* has been found (coming in at 37cm) but that is thought to have been a baby, whereas the microraptor fossil was a fully-grown adult.

- The largest dinosaur footprint discovered to date was found in Australia and is just over one and a half metres long. It is believed to have come from an *apatosaurus*.

- The fastest dinosaurs are believed to be *ornithomimosaurs*, which bore a striking resemblance to ostriches today. It is thought that they could run at speeds of up to 45 miles per hour.

- *Mamenchisaurus* had the longest neck of any dinosaur, the largest of which we have found is an amazing fourteen metres long.
- The dinosaur that has been given the longest scientific name is *micropachycephalosaurus*, which means 'small, thick-headed lizard'.
- The first ever dinosaur nest discovered was found by Roy Chapman Andrews in Mongolia in 1923. This was the first evidence found which supported the theory that dinosaurs laid eggs – a theory later confirmed when dinosaur eggs themselves were found.
- The biggest dinosaur we have ever found is called the *argentinasaurus*. It is believed to have been around 35 metres long, although we have found very little of its skeleton. There are notes dating back to 1877 regarding a bone which could have come from a larger dinosaur (which we have called *amphicoelias fragillimus*), but as the actual fossils were lost, a theory that it could have been an incredible sixty metres long has been disputed.

PHYSIOLOGY

- Meat-eating dinosaurs (sometimes called *therapods*, meaning 'beast-footed') had hooked claws on their toes for ripping flesh, whereas plant-eaters usually had blunt hooves.

- Therapods generally walked on two feet rather than four, which made them faster and helped them to catch prey with their arms.

- Some dinosaur skulls had large holes in them that made their heads lighter. This was especially important for larger dinosaurs, whose heads could be as big as a family car!

- It is thought that the reason many dinosaurs had long tails was to help with balance whilst running or standing up on their hind legs.

- Like lizards today, dinosaurs hatched their young from eggs. The largest eggs were the size of basketballs, and the smallest we have found are just 3cm in diameter.

- Dinosaurs can be divided into two groups. *Saurischian* means 'lizard-hips', and these dinosaurs had one hipbone pointing forward, whereas *ornithischian* dinosaurs had all hipbones pointing backwards like a bird, the word of course meaning 'bird-hipped'. Amazingly, scientists believe that the birds we know today actually evolved from saurischians and *not* ornithischians!

- The largest herbivores had to eat a ton of food every single day – an incredible volume of vegetation.

- Dinosaurs' eyes generally faced out on opposite sides of their heads (like a cow's eyes do) rather than both facing forwards (like a human's). This allowed them to see danger coming from a much wider angle.

- We believe that most dinosaurs had green and brown scaly skin which would have been effective camouflage amongst the trees and plants which made up their habitat.

- Some scientist believe that some dinosaurs would have shed their skin as they grew, just as snakes and lizards do today.

Interesting Dinosaurs

- *Deinonychus* – its name means 'terrible claw' and it was one of the most ferocious dinosaurs of the Cretaceous period. If you've seen *Jurassic Park*, what *they* call *velociraptors* were in fact examples of this beast!

- *Ultrasaurus* – a large dinosaur discovered in South Korea, however its provenance is in dispute, as some believe the bones found were misidentified... and were in fact those of a *supersaurus*.

- *Carnotaurus* – a similar dinosaur to *tyrannosaurus rex*, but thought to have been able to run at faster speeds, possibly making it even more deadly!

- *Euoplocephalus* – one of the largest species of anklyosaur, with an enormous club on the end of its tail.

- *Compsognathus* – a turkey-sized dinosaur covered with feathers which fed on a diet of small lizards.

- *Spinosaurus* – now thought to be the largest carnivorous dinosaur, eighteen metres in length and weighing in at over twenty tons.

- *Parasaurolophus* – a dinosaur with a huge, elaborate crest on its head; the purpose of which is still unknown, although scientists suggest it might have been for regulation of body temperature.

- *Sauroposeidon* – thought to be the tallest land animal ever to have existed at over 18 metres in height!

- *Gigantoraptor* – the largest feathered dinosaur discovered to date – eight metres long and weighing over two tons, it is an amazing 35 times bigger than the second largest found!
- *Archaeopteryx* – the transition between feathered dinosaurs and birds; the fossils of this species that have been discovered give us the strongest evidence of the Darwinian theory of evolution.

Did You Know?

- We aren't sure exactly how long an individual dinosaur would live for – although some palaeontologists say it is realistic that the larger species could have lived as long as 200 years!

- The first ever stegosaurus skeleton was found in Colorado, which is now known as the 'Stegosaurus State'!

- It is theorised that the majority of dinosaurs were no bigger than a man, however the larger ones were fossilized easier, so we don't see an 'even spread' of sizes when excavating.

- The first dinosaurs were carnivores (meaning they ate meat), whereas herbivores (who only ate plants) actually evolved later. In total, it is thought that there were more plant-eaters.

- Dinosaurs had hollow bones which are lighter than they look – just like birds do today.

- Some herbivores swallowed rocks which stayed in their stomachs and helped grind up food.

- Tyrannosaurus rex couldn't actually chew – it only had teeth for ripping flesh. Because of this it would swallow huge chunks of meat up to 500 pounds each!

- Scientists argue as to whether or not tyrannosaurus rex could run. Some believe it could reach speeds of up to 20 miles per hour, whereas others think that it was so unwieldy that it couldn't run at all!

- Both Argentina and China currently boast some of the best spots to find dinosaur fossils, and recently many extremely well-preserved examples have been found there.
- The dinosaurs with the shortest names are *mei* and *kol*, two feathered species discovered in China and Mongolia.

General Facts – Part 2

- There are a number of cases of different palaeontologists giving the same dinosaur different names. For instance, *brontosaurus* and *apatosaurus* are in fact the same species, and we have known this since 1911.

- You may picture the huge complete skeletons you have seen in museums as being the norm, however the sad truth is that most dinosaurs are identified from a single bone or tooth – and often more than half of those 'complete' skeletons in museums are actually made from plaster!

- Because birds today are descended from dinosaurs, some scientists believe that dinosaur meat tasted like chicken!

- You might wonder how two stegosauruses mated without hurting each other, with those big spiny plates on their backs... well, so do scientists! No definitive theory has been proposed, although options range from the female lying on her side whilst the male approaches upright to them both lying down belly-to-belly and shuffling together!

- Because of the fact that the young of many dinosaur species have skeletons quite different to their equivalent adults, it is now thought that up to a third of species named so far may not actually exist... rather they are younger examples of other correctly identified species!

- Fossilization is rare – but natural mummification is even rarer. Yet in 1999 a teenager called Tyler Lyson found a mummified hadrosaur in North Dakota. Palaeontologists have since been studying this incredible find, which has led to an amazing increase in our understanding of dinosaurs, including how they walked and what their skin looked like.

- There is a town in Colorado called Dinosaur, whose streets include *Triceratops Terrace*, *Cletisaurus Circle*, *Brontosaurus Boulevard* and *The Stegosaurus Freeway*!

- Chinese scientists have discovered flea-like creatures from the Jurassic era which would have clung on to the scaly skin of dinosaurs with powerful legs. They were much larger than fleas today, and even had long beaks that worked like the needle from a syringe, piercing the skin and sucking the dinosaur's blood!

- Dinosaurs have been found in 35 of America's 50 states.

- One incredible worldwide find was made in 1971 when palaeontologists discovered the fossilized remains of two dinosaurs trapped in battle! The velociraptor and the protoceratops were found in the Gobi desert in Mongolia.

Well-Known Prehistoric Creatures

- ***Tyrannosaurus rex*** – one of the last dinosaurs to evolve before the mass extinction event, T. rex ranks amongst the largest land predators the world has ever seen.

- ***Dimetrodon*** – living around 290 million years ago, this reptile in fact became extinct before the first true dinosaurs even evolved!

- ***Ankylosaurus*** – considered the archetypal armoured dinosaur, nine metres long and weighing six tonnes. It was covered in horns and plates of bone and had a club on the end of its tail.

- ***Triceratops*** – distinctive three-horned dinosaur which was hunted by the tyrannosaurus rex.

- ***Pteranodon*** – not a dinosaur but a flying reptile, it had a wingspan of over six metres. We have discovered around 1200 fossilized examples, many almost perfectly preserved.

- ***Stegosaurus*** – one of the most recognisable dinosaurs, nine metres long with huge armoured plates rising vertically from its back. Scientists believe these may have been a form of defense, or perhaps used to regulate body temperature.

- ***Plesiosaurus*** – again, not a dinosaur but a water-based reptile. It has been suggested that if the legends of sea and lake monsters are true, they could have evolved directly from this species... although scientists will tell you this is highly unlikely!

- *Diplodocus* – long dinosaur with sturdy legs; easily recognisable and for many years was thought to be the longest dinosaur that existed.

- *Brachiosaurus* – with its front legs longer than its hind legs, this sauropod had the stance of a giraffe – also having a similarly long neck and relatively short tail for its order.

- *Velociraptor* – although the name was popularised by Jurassic park, the dinosaurs featured in the film were actually of the species *deinonychus*. Actual velociraptors were smaller feathered creatures which attacked prey with a claw on their hind foot.

The Most Amazing Facts

- Although we consider the first discovery of dinosaur fossils to be in 1822, some bones were in fact found prior to this – around 300 years ago, people believed they came from elephants or even giant humans, whereas when some dinosaur teeth were discovered in China 3500 years ago, people thought they belonged to a dragon!

- Most dinosaurs had a single body opening for urination, defecation and reproduction; however some did have separate organs. Some scientist think that the tyrannosaurus rex had a penis over three and a half metres in length!

- We have discovered fossilized trackways in Australia. At first it was thought this was evidence of a stampede of dinosaurs running away from a massive carnivore, however recent research suggests that it may be the site of a river crossing!

- Dinosaurs were not in fact the first reptiles to rule the earth! *Archosaurs* ('ruling lizards') and *therapsids* (mammal-like reptiles) were the original kings of the land until around the beginning of the Jurassic period.

- Contrary to what you may think, there were a number of mammals around in the time of the dinosaurs. *Repenomamus* for instance was one of the largest – about a metre long, and enjoyed a diet of small dinosaurs. We know this because one repenomamus fossil has been found with the remains of a *psittacosaurus* in its stomach!

- Over half of all of the species of dinosaur identified have been found in the last 20 years or so!

- A new species of dinosaur discovered in 2006 was named after the famous wizarding school in Harry Potter – dracorex hogwartsia, literally *the Hogwarts Dragon!*

- The stegosaurus lived around 156 million years ago, whereas the tyrannosaurus rex lived around 67 million years ago. This means that the T-rex lived closer in time to us than it did to the stegosaurus! Amazing!

- The first dinosaur in space – that we know of – was a maiasaura fossil taken on a space shuttle mission in 1985, although no-one from NASA has given a scientific explanation as to why...

- Sadly, although it seems reasonable, the science of *Jurassic Park* isn't going to bring dinosaurs back. Unfortunately, DNA degrades over time, and is not thought to last more than 1.5 million years at the most. This means that even the most perfectly preserved specimen from the finest and most secure piece of amber will not have any DNA left to clone from. However, that doesn't mean there aren't other methods of bringing dinosaurs into the modern world!

And Finally...

- The dinosaurs actually became extinct before either the Rocky Mountains or the Alps were even formed!

101 Amazing Facts about Dogs

The Basics

- The word *dog* is believed to come from the old English word *docga*, which was a particular canine breed.

- Dogs are often referred to as 'man's best friend' because of their long history of being companion animals to humans over thousands of years.

- It is estimated that there are around five hundred million dogs in the world, with the United States being the country that is home to the most.

- There are hundreds of different breeds of dog, many of them specialising in particular tasks such as hunting, security, and assisting those with a disability such as blindness.

- In canine terminology, a male is usually known as a *dog*, and a female a *bitch*. A *puppy* usually refers to a dog or bitch who is less than one year old.

- A group of offspring is called a *litter*, with the mother being called the *dam* and the father the *sire*.

- Most breeds today are relatively new – usually no more than a few hundred years old, and some much more recent. They have generally been created by selective breeding, choosing the dogs and bitches with particular traits to breed with each other.

- The average lifespan of a dog is around twelve years, however some breeds sadly don't live this long, whereas others enjoy much longer lives.

- In England in the fourteenth century, *dog* actually referred to a particular type of *hound*, which was the word used to describe all domesticated canines. Over time however, the word 'dog' took over as referring to any breed, whereas 'hound' specifically related to hunting dogs.

- Although dogs have always been kept for working purposes, today it is more common to keep a dog for companionship. Whereas in times gone past, this practice would have been reserved for the rich and the social elite, today many people take up the opportunity to welcome a dog into their family life.

A Poodle

Health

- Dogs only have sweat glands in-between their paws, whereas humans sweat from all over their bodies. The only other way a dog can release heat is by panting.

- Different sized dogs require different amounts of exercise and it is important for you to understand what yours needs. Without the proper lifestyle, a dog will quickly display behavioural and health issues.

- When bathing your dog you should use special dog shampoo – products designed for humans can contain irritants that will harm your dog's skin.

- It is wise to regularly brush your dog's teeth; this is because it limits the risk of it picking up oral diseases and allows you to spot future teeth and gum problems much easier.

- You should <u>never</u> feed your dog grapes or raisins as they can cause liver failure. You must also ensure they don't consume apple or pear seeds because these contain quantities of arsenic that can be deadly to dogs.

- Similarly, you must avoid feeding your dog chocolate or anything that contains caffeine, as they do not have the ability to process certain chemicals effectively.

- It is also unwise to allow your dog to drink milk, as most breeds are lactose intolerant.

- A healthy dog usually has a temperature of between 101 and 102.5 degrees Fahrenheit.

- It is possible to estimate a dog breed's potential lifespan by the shape of their faces. Flat faced breeds tend to live shorter lives, whereas those with long snouts often live to a much older age.

- When a puppy is born it has no teeth and cannot see or hear.

A Dalmatian

Dogs in History

- Images of dogs have been found in Spanish cave paintings dating back over ten thousand years.

- *The Epic of Gilgamesh* (considered one of the earliest surviving works of literature) describes how the goddess Innana had seven prized hunting dogs.

- Dogs are almost always described as loyal companions in ancient literature. One famous example is in Homer's epic *Odyssey* where he describes how Odysseus returns home having been away for twenty years and yet his faithful dog Argos still recognises him.

- The ancient city of Peritas was founded by Alexander the Great and was named in memory of his favourite dog.

- Many people know that the ancient Egyptians worshipped cats, but did you also know they revered their pet dogs? When one would die the family would shave their eyebrows off and smear mud in their hair as a sign of morning.

- Tomb paintings of the famous pharaoh Ramses the Great depict him with hunting dogs; when he died it is likely that they were buried with him as it was believed they would offer him loyalty and companionship in the afterlife.

- The ancient Mbaya Indians held a belief that humans once lived underground – until the dogs dug us up.

- It is thought that the Mongolian emperor Kublai Khan owned more than five thousand dogs, most of them mastiffs!
- The Chinese believe that people born in the year of the dog are loyal and discreet but can be temperamental. The Mayans and Aztecs believed that to be born under the sign of the dog meant you might become a great leader.
- Large dogs such as Mastiffs and Great Danes have historically been used in battle; in medieval times they were even known to have worn spiked collars and even suits of armour.

A Dachshund

Behaviour

- A dog curls up into a ball when it is sleeping due to an inbuilt genetic behaviour – the position is designed to keep the dog warm and to protect its abdomen (and therefore vital organs) from predators.

- When your dog's paw is twitching when it is asleep, it really is dreaming! Scientists have discovered that dogs have the same stages of sleep as humans, and when they are in the REM (Rapid Eye Movement) stage, this is when they dream.

- Even an average dog can learn the meaning of around one hundred and fifty different words – that's about as many as a two-year-old child!

- Dogs are natural predators. Due to this, it is very hard to change an aggressive behaviour that your dog picked up. With this in mind you should always try to train your dog not to bite from a young age, as this will be much easier than stopping it from biting once it has developed the habit.

- When teaching a dog spoken instructions, it will learn much quicker if the command is stated in conjunction with a physical gesture.

- The reason that a male dog lifts its leg up whilst urinating is that it wants other dogs to think it is tall (and therefore not to be messed with!). Amazingly, a behaviour has been observed in wild dogs whereby they run up tree trunks whilst relieving themselves so that they appear huge!

- Dogs often chase their tails – and for a variety of positive and negative reasons, such as curiosity, anxiety or even just exercise. However, if your dog seems to spend a great deal of time exhibiting this behaviour, you should take it to a vet.

- It is probably not a wise idea smile at a dog; most will consider this 'baring of teeth' an act of aggression.

- Even today, dogs are 'pack animals' and see their owners as part of their group – usually (although not always) the 'top dog'. When there is more than one dog in a household, there will be a pretty strict pecking order!

- If your dog is scratching its ears for longer than normal, this could be a sign of a variety of ailments including fleas, ear mites or a yeast infection. As with any noticeable alteration in behaviour it should be checked out by a vet.

A Collie

Did You Know?

- The Germans are thought to be the first in modern times to train guide dogs for the blind; after the first world war many soldiers were left blinded by gas attacks and the government began a programme of supplying canine assistants to them.

- Guide dogs are actually trained to be disobedient – but only if they believe one of their owner's commands is unsafe.

- It is thought that dogs enjoy squeaky toys because they sound a little like an injured animal (such as a field mouse), something that awakens a dog's natural genetic hunting instinct.

- The phrase *raining cats and dogs* is believed to come from England a few hundred years ago when after a severe storm, stray cats and dogs would sadly drown and float down the street as the water drained away – this gave the impression that they had fallen from the sky along with the rain.

- Animal behaviouralists now believe that the reason a dog so enjoys sticking its head out of a moving car window is that it gets an exciting overload of smells, and has been compared to the experience of a human going from watching a standard definition TV to visiting a huge IMAX cinema screen!

- In an American study it was found that the most common dog names were Max and Jake (for males) and Maggie and Molly (for females).

- It's not just humans that find yawning contagious – if one dog in a pack yawns, it is likely the other will also follow.

- All pure border collies today can trace their ancestry back to a single dog – Old Hemp, who was born in September 1893 and died in May 1902.

- In a survey, a third of dog owners said that they leave messages to their dogs on their answering machines when they are away, or even talk to them over the phone if someone is there to help!

- The religion of Zoroastrianism which is believed to be followed by more than two million people worldwide has a detailed section in one of its religious texts entirely dedicated to the breeding and care of dogs.

A Rhodesian Ridgeback

Biology

- Whereas a cat laps up water from the *top* of its tongue, a dog in fact forms the *back* of theirs into the shape of a cup, and draws water into its mouth this way!

- A dog's noseprint is as unique as your fingerprint.

- It is a myth that dogs only see in black and white – they do in fact see in colour, although we do not know if they perceive different wavelengths of light in the same way that we do.

- Dogs have excellent eyesight in some situations. Although one cannot usually see you if you stand still at a distance of just a couple of hundred metres, if you are a mile away and waving your arms, your dog will recognise you right away!

- A dog can hear sounds that are four times further away than an average human can perceive.

- Of course, dogs have an excellent sense of smell. Whereas a human has around five million cells that detect scents, an average dog has an incredible two hundred and twenty million. Even the part of the brain that processes smell signals is four times larger in a dog than in a human. All of this combined means that your dog has a sense of smell around one hundred thousand times better than yours!

- A dog's urine tells another canine a great deal about its owner, including what sex it is, how old it is, how healthy it is and even if it is happy or sad.

- A bitch's pregnancy usually lasts around sixty days.

- The shoulder blades of a dog are not connected to the rest of their skeleton, which allows them to be more flexible when running.
- In addition to their upper and lower eyelids, dogs also have a third lid on each eye, known as a *nictitating membrane* (or a 'haw') which helps to protect the eye and keep it moist.

A Greyhound

Record Breakers

- The heaviest dog ever to have lived is believed to be Zorba, an English Mastiff who weighed an incredible 343 pounds in 1989.

- During the 2009 X Games in Los Angeles, an English Bulldog called Tillman propelled himself one hundred metres on a skateboard in just 19.68 seconds.

- The tallest dog ever to have lived was called Giant George; he was a Great Dane who lived with his owner in Tucson, Arizona and measured an incredible 43 inches at the withers. He sadly died in October 2013.

- The smallest adult living dog in the world (in 2014) was declared as Miracle Milly, a Chihuahua who measures just 3.8 inches from backbone to paw.

- A Basset hound called Mr Jeffries holds the record for the dog with the longest ears – his measured an amazing 29.2 cm each!

- The fastest domestic dog breed is believed to be the Greyhound, which can reach speeds of up to 45 mph in a straight line.

- The dog with the longest tongue ever measured was a Boxer by the name of Brandy. Her tongue was an incredible seventeen inches long!

- The highest recorded jump that a dog has ever cleared in competition was 68 inches tall – it was conquered by Cinderella May the Greyhound.

- The world's oldest dog was an incredible 29 years and five months old when he died in 1939. Bluey was an Australian Cattle Dog who worked with cattle and sheep for most of his long, happy life.
- One unusual record belongs to Anastasia the Jack Russell, who is famous for popping 100 balloons in the shortest amount of time – just 44.49 seconds!

A Chihuahua

Dog Breeds

- The Dachshund (or sausage dog) has is unusual shape for a reason – the breed was originally bred to burrow into badgers' sets and fight them!

- Just like human babies, Chihuahuas are born with a molera – a soft spot – on the back of their skulls which closes up with age. They are thought to be the only breed that displays this physical trait.

- Pekingese dogs were worshipped in China many years ago, and were considered so valuable that they were usually only owned by kings and emperors who would often allocate them their own servant.

- It is thought that the Greyhound is the world's oldest identifiable breed of dog, and dates back around nine thousand years. The *grey* in the name doesn't refer to a colour, but is from the German word *greis* which actually means 'ancient'.

- The Poodle is actually believed to be a German rather than a French breed. Historians think that hunters would shave much of the breed's hair off so they could swim better and faster, but would leave hair around their joints so they still kept warm.

- When Dalmatians are born they are completely white.

- The Newfoundland is exceptionally at home in the water. Not only is its coat water resistant but it even has webbed feet! It is thought that they were bred this way to help haul nets for fishermen.

- The Labrador is the most popular dog breed in both the United Kingdom and America.
- The Border Collie and the Poodle are believed to be two of the most intelligent dog breeds, whilst the least intelligent are often said to be the Basenji and the Afghan Hound.
- The Rhodesian Ridgeback was amazingly used to hunt lions in Rhodesia (now Zimbabwe) in the nineteenth century, and Dogo Argentinos were bred to hunt South American jaguars!

A St. Bernard

Evolution

- Dogs today are descended from an animal called the *Miacis* which lived around forty million years ago.

- The Miacis in fact evolved into another animal called the *Tormarctus*, which itself later evolved into the genus *Canis*.

- It is believed that dogs actually first domesticated themselves; when humans began to build settlements around fifteen thousand years ago, wolves were attracted to these sources of food, warmth and comfort and evolved their behaviour to be friendly towards humans.

- The humans of the time are thought to have 'accepted' the wolves into their communities as they would have been extremely useful for hunting.

- Amazingly, we now think dogs were domesticated before horses, chickens, sheep, cats, goats and even cattle.

- We believe that initially, younger wolves (even perhaps young babies) would have been the first to interact with humans. Over time, people would have bred them – or at least 'allowed' them to breed.

- Over a few thousand years this would have happened, with the people in the community killing any offspring that showed the more violent or aggressive tendencies that wolves can display. Thus a form of selective breeding occurred and over time the wolves that lived around these settlements became very different to those that stuck to the wild.

- This process would have happened in many communities, not just one. Each settlement would have hunted in a slightly different way due to their environment, and the wolves – now essentially dogs – would have developed to reflect this.

- It is then thought that humans from various settlements began to trade with each other; dogs would certainly have been traded, with specimens being chosen for their particular qualities and suitability.

- From this, the many different types of dogs evolved: Scent hounds, sight hounds, working and sporting dogs, terriers and more would all have been selectively bred to assist humans with various tasks.

A Schnauzer

The Most Amazing Facts

- Historians have found evidence that in medieval times, mongrels that belonged to peasants had to wear heavy blocks around their necks to stop them running free and thus breeding with noblemen's purebred hunting dogs!

- In Russia, some stray dogs have demonstrated fantastic levels of intelligence and ingenuity by learning how to use the subway system to travel around Moscow in their search for food!

- Plenty of people know that the first mammal to orbit the earth was a Russian dog by the name of Laika. But few are aware that Laika's daughter (called Pushnika) bred with John F Kennedy's terrier (called Charlie) and the two had four puppies together!

- A scientist by the name of Doctor Roger Mugford made a device called a 'wagometer' which he claimed could interpret a dog's mood simply by analysing the wagging of its tail!

- Welsh folklore states that corgis are in fact the dogs of the fairies and elves, and are used not just to pull the little folk's coaches but also as the steeds of their greatest warriors!

- Amazingly, wild baboons have been seen kidnapping puppies from their families, and taking care of them throughout their lives. They become part of the baboon's own family, their duty usually being as a protective guard dog!

A Labrador

- By studying documents we have found out what the ancient Egyptians called their dogs. Generally they had names that described their colour or their best skills, such as 'blackie', 'brave one', or 'good herdsman'.

- It has been proven that dogs can detect lung cancer by smelling a patient's breath, and can even sense early signs of cancer before medical experts can detect them.

- When a number of lampposts fell over in Croatia, people thought there might be a group of vandals about or that they weren't constructed very well... however it turned out that a chemical in dogs' urine was reacting with the metal they were made from, causing it to weaken and rot!

- Lord Byron was so annoyed that his tutors at Cambridge University would not allow him to bring his dog to live with him that he brought along a bear instead!

And Finally...

- In 1923, a family took their dog called Bobbie on a road trip from Oregon to Indiana. Sadly whilst they were there, Bobbie was separated from his owners and they couldn't find him anywhere. Saddened to have lost their loyal pet, they returned home. Amazingly however, six months later, Bobbie turned up at their door, having trekked nearly three thousand miles on his own to be reunited with his family.

An English Springer Spaniel

101 Amazing Facts about Lizards

The Basics

- Lizards are a group of reptiles that belong to the order *squamata*.

- In addition to lizards, the squamata order also contains snakes, and is the third-largest order of vertebrates after birds and fish. Squamata are defined as 'reptiles with overlapping scales'.

- Unusually, lizards are essentially defined as *any species of the order squamata that isn't a snake*. The only exception to this is the *tuatara*, a reptile that lives in New Zealand which is given a group all of its own!

- The key difference between lizards and snakes is that lizards *generally* have eyelids and external ears – although, confusingly, not *all* of them have both. Interestingly, you cannot separate the groups by having (or not having) legs, as there are some legless species of lizard. It is therefore not *always* possible to tell what is a snake and what is a lizard with just a quick look, even for an expert in the field.

- There are thought to be around six thousand different species of lizard alive today.

- Lizards live on every continent on the planet except for Antarctica.

- All lizards – like the vast majority of other reptiles – are cold-blooded. Leatherback turtles are one of the very few reptiles alive today that are an exception.

- Smaller lizards generally survive on a diet of insects such as flies and crickets, with slightly larger species eating other tiny creatures such as caterpillars, spiders and snails.

- The larger the lizard, the larger the prey, with one exception: the Iguana. Whereas other lizards are carnivorous, the Iguana is a herbivore and climbs trees to seek out the fruits and berries on which it survives.

- The very largest lizard, the *Komodo dragon*, has a special kind of bacteria in its saliva that paralyses its prey. This means that either an individual or a group can even bring down large animals such as pigs, deer and even cattle. Amazingly, it has been known for a Komodo dragon to target, kill and eat humans!

Thorny Devil

Biology

- Just like snakes, lizards 'smell' the air with their tongues.

- Most lizards have excellent colour vision; unsurprisingly as a result of this, colour is sometimes used by lizards as a means of communication.

- A number of species carry beautiful patterns on their undersides. These are used to communicate with other members of their species about territorial rights and even mating interests, but (being on their bellies) can be hidden from predators – it wouldn't be a good idea to have bright colours on display all the time, making the owner highly visible!

- Some lizards have a *dewlap* – a flap of skin underneath their throats which can be extended (using the *hyoid bone*) which is also a means of communication.

- Rather than a nose, lizards possess a *vomeronasal organ*, also called a *Jacobsen's organ*. The way it can be thought of working is that it almost 'tastes' the air. When a lizard flutters and wobbles its throat, it is actually passing air over this organ to better sense the air.

- With the exception of chameleons and agamids, all lizards lose their first set of teeth and grow a second just like you and I do.

- Some species of lizard lay eggs, whereas others give birth to live young. The eggs are usually soft as opposed to hard-shelled.

- Lizards are covered with scales that are made from *keratin* – this is the same material from which your hair and fingernails are made.

- Amazingly, some lizards have a structure with a lens and retina on top of their heads which controls hormone production when basking for heat; this can actually be thought of as a third eye, although it doesn't 'see' in the conventional sense.

- A significant number of lizard species can change their colour, allowing them to blend in better with surroundings.

Broadhead Skink

Record Breakers

- The largest lizard ever recorded in the wild was (of course) a *Komodo dragon*. Measuring 3.13 metres long, it weighed an incredible 166 kilograms!

- The fastest lizard observed to date is a *ctenosaura* (a type of *iguana*) that reached nearly 22mph in one measured burst of running.

- The rarest lizard alive today is thought to be the *Jamaican iguana*. We had actually believed that it was extinct – until a living specimen was discovered in 1990! Since then, only around one hundred individuals have been seen, putting it on the list of the most critically endangered species on the planet.

- The largest *true* lizards ever to have lived were the *mosasaurs*; these were marine species which could grow to an astonishing seventeen metres in length!

- According to one news report, the oldest bearded lizard in captivity lived to the grand old age of fourteen years. His owner said he drank a few sips of Guinness every day – although this is *not* recommended if you're planning on keeping a lizard of your own!

- The title of 'smallest lizard in the world' is currently shared between four different species – *Brookesia confidens, Brookesia desperata, Brookesia micra* and *Brookesia tristis*. These leaf chameleons when fully grown reach just 15mm in length and were found on the island of Madagascar in 2012.

- The oldest fossil of a lizard-like creature found so far was discovered in Germany and dates back 240 million years to the Middle Triassic period.

- Except for the Komodo dragon, the most venomous lizard is the *gila monster*. Unusually, its teeth have grooves that conduct the flow of venom into its victim when chewing it, rather than through one initial bite.

- The most recently discovered monitor lizard (at the time of writing) was a previously unknown species called the *Northern Sierra Madre forest monitor*. Found on the Philippine island of Luzon in 2009, *varanus bitatawa* (its official name) is brightly coloured, more than two metres long, and unusually for a monitor is herbivorous.

- Finally, a man from Bolivia who claims to be 123 years old – making him the oldest person ever to have lived – says that he has survived to such an age from living on a diet of lizards and foxes. Nice!

Brookesia Micra

Did You Know?

- Most lizards hibernate during the cold winter months.

- Although you think of lizards as coming out in the daytime to bask in the sunlight, those that live in the desert (such as the *ground gecko*) bury themselves in the sand during the day, and only come out at night when the sun has gone down.

- Although most lizards have four legs, some have just two, and some species have none at all!

- Geckos are a particularly diverse *infraorder* of lizards that are generally found in warm climates all over the world. One of their key distinguishing features is that they have no eyelids, and therefore lick their eyes in order to keep them clean and moist.

- Generally, lizards are nervous and skittish around humans, although there are some species which aren't so wary and it is these that tend to make better pets.

- Whereas many species of lizard are well adapted for climbing trees, there are a number that have evolved to burrow underground.

- Chameleons can move each eye independently, with their brains able to process what they are seeing – even when it is in two directions at the same time! This is fantastic for avoiding predators... and of course for spotting their next meal.

- Each species of lizard has adapted their scales to the environment in which they live. Some have tough scales to deal with bites from predators, whereas others such as skinks have smooth scales so that mud doesn't cling to them.

- Chameleons' upper and lower eyelids are joined together, with only a tiny hole left open for them to see through.
- Lizards keep growing throughout their entire lives.

Gila Monster

Unusual Species

- The *toadhead agama lizard* communicates to others of its species by curling and uncurling its tail – but this is not the only out-of-the-ordinary thing it does with its body. Amazingly, it has some bizarre mouth flaps which it fully opens when faced with a predator. The highly colourful (and frankly quite frightening) look generally scares them away!

- Not only does the *gila monster* have an amazing name, but it is also considered one of the most venomous lizards on the planet; it injects its prey with a toxin delivered through grooves in its razor-sharp teeth.

- If there was a competition for the most beautifully coloured lizard, the *panther chameleon* would certainly reach the final stages. Possessing a green body with dark vertical stripes, bright blue spots, red-tinted legs and tail, white mouth and a blue-highlighted ridge to its back, this wonderful species is even suitable to be kept as a pet if you are an experienced owner.

- The *frill lizard* has a ruff-like flap of skin around its neck that it extends to scare off predators (and which is also used as during its mating ritual). Not only this, but it also runs upright on its two back legs. If you're looking for a lizard alive today that most closely resembles something from Jurassic Park, then this is it!

- The *horned toad lizard* has a really rather nasty defence mechanism. If a predator approaches too closely, it deliberately builds up blood pressure in its head, until the vessels around its eyes explode, squirting streams of foul-tasting blood onto the would-be attacker. If this happened to you, would *you* continue to attack?

- The *Brookesia minima* is one of the smallest reptiles on the planet; even when fully grown, this miniature chameleon can perch on your fingertip.

- The *flying gecko* can not only scale surfaces as smooth as glass (due to a special feature allowing its toes to grip any surface at a molecular level), but it also extends flaps of skin to allow it to glide skilfully between tree branches!

- You'd have to be pretty awesome to risk eating a crocodile, right? Yet that is exactly what the *Nile monitor* does every day. Admittedly it only targets the young crocodiles, however as they can grow up to three metres in length, it *can* even give the adults a run for their money! Frighteningly, Nile monitors have been sold as pets in the past – although they come with a warning to be kept away from babies and cats!

- The *thorny devil lizard* is (as you may guess) covered in sharp thorns. However it appears this doesn't completely deter all predators, as it has one additional – and amazing – line of defence. On its back it has a decoy head in the hope that if it does get bitten, it will be this slightly less vital area!

- If you venture to the Galapagos Islands, you may well see the *marine iguanas* that live on the shoreline and live purely on a diet of green algae that they scrape from underwater rocks. The reason they make this list of notable species however is due to the fact that Charles Darwin was totally repulsed by the sight of these lizards, referring to them as 'imps of darkness'!

Yemen Chameleon

INTERESTING FACTS

- Palaeontologists think that there have been lizards on the earth for more than two hundred million years!

- There are four generally recognised suborders of lizard; these are the *Iguania, Gekkota, Amphisbaenia* and *Autarchoglossa*.

- Interestingly, no-one is *really* sure in which of these four suborders the *blind skinks* should be classed.

- One unnerving ability that lizards possess is that they can keep incredibly still for hours on end. This actually helps them avoid predators, as some tend to hunt their prey based on movement.

- Most lizards have the ability to defend themselves from the moment they are born – although obviously to a lesser extent than their much larger parents!

- A number of species of lizard have developed an unusual ability – they can actually detach their tail if it happens to be caught by a predator.

- Furthermore, a lizard will commonly return to the location in which they detached their tail in the hope that at least some of it is still there – so they can eat it! It is common for lizards to store nutrients in their tails which they can then eat if times are tough... and one should never let a nutritious meal go to waste.

- Even more amazingly, they can grow another tail in its place – although this replacement is made from cartilage rather than bone.

- Lizards shed their skin (or 'molt') as they grow, although it tends to come off in pieces. One exception to this however is the *alligator lizard*, which sheds its entire skin in one piece – just like a snake!
- Although lizards spend a great deal of their time basking in the sun, overheating can be a problem – and so it is common for species in certain climates to hide away during the very hottest period of the day.

Frill Necked Lizard

The Komodo Dragon

- The Komodo dragon is the world's largest species of lizard.

- They can be found in just one place on earth: Komodo National Park, a series of three large and twenty-six small islands in Indonesia. Only the large islands are inhabited by these magnificent beasts.

- On the islands, the 'dragons' can be found in a wide variety of habitats, from dense forests and open plains to sandy beaches and mangrove swamps.

- Komodo dragons are in fact a type of *monitor lizard*; most monitor species (of which there are currently 73) are large, however the smallest grow to just 20cm in length.

- The existence of the Komodo dragon was not widely known to humans until 1910, when a Dutch explorer led an expedition to find a rumoured 'land crocodile'. He captured and killed a specimen, much to the amazement of the scientific community at the time.

- It is thought that sadly there are fewer than six thousand Komodo dragons left on the planet.

- Amazingly, young Komodo dragons spend their early years living in trees – however as they grow they become too heavy to climb safely, and thus live a life on terra firma.

- According to keepers at Washington D.C.'s national zoo, Komodo dragons recognise their handlers, and each one has a distinct personality.

- Scientists theorise that the reason this particular species has evolved to such an extraordinary size is that the islands they inhabit are not home to any other similarly-sized carnivorous animals; this evolutionary process is known as *island gigantism*.

- Komodo dragons do enter the water, as long as there's a good chance of grabbing themselves a meal – though being cold-blooded, they can quickly become sluggish in the water due to its cooling effect on their bodies. Individuals can swim over half a kilometre, and dive almost five metres under the surface.

Komodo Dragon

Keeping Lizards as Pets

- If you decide to keep a lizard as a pet, make sure you are *fully* committed to the idea. Any pet is a significant commitment, and a lizard will be with you for many years.

- Although many lizards are cheap to buy, the equipment to properly look after them can be much more costly. Look into everything that you will need (not just initially but also on an ongoing basis) to ensure you can afford it.

- Many insurers will offer cover for lizards; again this is a wise choice as when you are worrying about helping a sick pet find its way back to full health, you don't want to be fretting about how to cover the cost of doing so.

- Whilst a lizard may be small initially, consider how large an individual can grow. For instance, iguanas may be cute when they are first born, but they can reach up to six feet in length as asults – do you have the space for this?

- Once you have decided that a lizard is the right pet for you, speak to an expert about what breed is most suitable for a beginner. Although you may want a certain species right away, it may be best to first learn how to care for a species more suitable for first-time owners.

- Enjoy spending time with your lizard. Show it plenty of affection and it will be a very rewarding pet!

- It would be wise to identify a vet near you who specialises in lizards. At some point during your lizard's life it is likely to need medical attention, and it is a wise move to know where you will go for this well in advance.

- Try to source your lizard from a reputable breeder who can supply you with a captive-bred individual. Those caught from the wild tend to be more stressed in captivity, as well as being more prone to disease.

- Lizards can often carry harmful bacteria such as salmonella. It is therefore extremely important to have a strict hygiene routine in place; make sure you know how best to minimise the risks associated with these bacteria.

- It is best to avoid feeding your lizard food caught in the wild, as insects you find locally may have parasites – and it would not be a good idea to introduce these into the food chain. You may find it best to breed and raise crickets or mealworms at home; there are plenty of guides online that will help you do this.

Iguana

Myths & Legend

- There is a belief known as *lizard astrology* (or *gowli panchangam*) that tells of how a lizard falling onto various parts of your body signifies different things; for instance if one falls onto your shoulder, you will overcome an opponent, whereas if one falls onto your back you will soon succumb to bad luck. It goes without saying that this is about as true as any *other* form of astrology..!

- Ancient West African belief held that chameleons were able to fetch fire from the sun.

- Lizards have been considered in the past to possess magical properties; think of the witches' potion in Shakespeare's *Macbeth*: 'Adder's fork, and blind-worm's sting, lizard's leg, and owlet's wing'...

- An Australian Aboriginal belief holds that the sky would fall if you killed a lizard.

- There are legends and tales of dragons in almost every culture across the world. It is thought that *some* of these beliefs can be attributed to large lizards – although scientists have actually proposed that there were *actual* dragons many thousands of years ago, and we just haven't found their remains yet!

- In early Christianity, the chameleon was used to symbolize the devil, who could change his appearance to deceive mankind.

- Both the ancient Egyptians and Greeks saw the lizard as a symbol of wisdom and good fortune.

- In legend, the Salamander is portrayed as having the ability to live in flames (in fact, sometimes even needing fire to survive) – however *real* salamanders are in fact amphibians and not reptiles.

- In some Native American tribes, lizards were associated with survival; a new-born baby's umbilical cord would be sewn into an amulet in the shape of a lizard!

- The Pomo Indians believe that a lizard was one of five creators of the universe, who made humans in their combined image.

Panther Chameleon

The Most Amazing Facts

- A 1926 expedition by W Douglas Burden to the Komodo Islands was in fact the inspiration for the 1933 movie *King Kong*! As a side note, the expedition was successful and Burden brought back no fewer than twelve preserved Komodo dragons and two live ones.

- Some species of lizard (including *basilisks*) run purely using their hind legs. Some are so quick and delicate of foot that they can run across the surface of the water – this has led to those of the genus basilisk being called *Jesus lizards!*

- Chameleons catch their prey by quickly projecting their tongues far out of their mouths; the target instantly becomes stuck to the lizard's tongue which is then quickly retracted. Amazingly, some of the smaller species of chameleon can extend their tongues over twice their body length!

- In Central America, the *green iguana* is a served as a traditional dish; there it is also known as the 'chicken of the tree'. Similarly, there are nomadic African tribes who eat *spiny-tailed lizards* which they call 'fish of the desert'!

- The *Caiman lizard* lives on a diet of snails, which it eats with absolute precision. It tips the snail to the back of its mouth where it carefully cracks the shell with its molar-like teeth. It then gradually rotates its tasty morsel, extracting the juicy morsel and ejecting the broken pieces of shell out of its mouth!

- Amazingly, scientists have found some species that have evolved from laying eggs to giving birth to live young – for instance the *yellow-bellied three-toed skink* in Australia.

- Many lizards that live in trees have a *prehensile tail* – this means that it is used to grasp at a branch just like a hand can; this allows for excellent balance.

- The *tropical girdled lizard* has a rather unique defence mechanism. When it is in danger of attack, it runs into a crack in a nearby rock, and inflates its body like a balloon. By doing this it becomes lodged in so tight that a predator can't pull it out!

- Although it is commonly known that the word *dinosaur* means 'terrible lizard', dinosaurs were not in fact true lizards – however they are very close in evolutionary terms, and share many features.

- Some lizards do not just change their colour to blend in with their surroundings; it can also be a way of communicating their mood to other lizards!

And Finally...

- If you are interested in buying a lizard as a pet, you should do plenty of research before deciding which species would suit you best.

Sand Lizard

101 Amazing Facts about Insects

...and other arthropods

General Facts

- Insects are part of the phylum *Arthropoda*, meaning 'jointed leg'. They are just one class of arthropod, others of which include *arachnids* and *crustaceans*.

- Arthropods are in fact divided into four subgroups – *chelicerates* (spiders, mites, scorpions etc.), *crustaceans* (lobsters, crabs, shrimp, woodlice etc.), *hexapods* (insects and others with a head, thorax and abdomen) and *myriapods* (millipedes, centipedes etc.).

- Arthropods are cold-blooded.

- All Arthropods have segmented bodies.

- Insects are believed to represent an incredible ninety per cent of all of the life on earth.

- There are believed to be between six and ten million species of insect on our planet.

- Insects have three parts to their body – the head, thorax and abdomen.

- They also have two antennae and three pairs of legs.

- Insects usually go through four life stages: egg, larvae, pupa and adult.

- Arachnids are a type of arthropod which have eight legs.

Honey Bees

- The honey bee is the only insect that produces food eaten by humans.

- A colony of honey bees consists of between 20,000 and 60,000 individuals.

- It takes the pollen from around two million flowers to make just half a kilogram of honey.

- As bees go through their lives, they take on different job roles – from cleaning out their cells when they are very young to feeding larvae as they grow older, performing guard duty through their mid-lives, and finally as fully-fledged adults going out to collect pollen.

- Although bees generally die when they sting humans (due to the barb in their sting getting caught under our skin, which rips it out of their bodies), they can quite happily sting other animals without harming themselves.

- Honey bees make honey by combining nectar from flowers with enzymes from glands in their mouths. They store this mixture in honeycombs until much of the water has been evaporated, then worker bees cap off the honeycombs. This means that when the bees need the food (such as in the winter when nectar can't be found naturally) they can uncap it and tuck in.

- A beehive always has one queen who is the sole female responsible for reproducing. She lays around two thousand eggs per day.

- Queen bees all have different personalities, and amazingly this influences the personality of the entire hive. Some are aggressive, others are passive and some are much harder working than others!

- Male honey bees are called drones and are purely responsible for mating with the queen – they have no stinger and do no other work.

- Worker bees are always female. In the course of her lifetime, a single worker bee will produce around one twelfth of a teaspoon of honey.

Amazing Arthropods

- A normal housefly can beat its wings around two hundred times a second! It is a midge however that holds the record for the fastest wingbeat at more than one thousand times a second!

- The millipede *illacme plenipes* holds the record for the animal with the most legs – 750 in total!

- The termite supposedly has the smelliest fart in the entire animal kingdom!

- The rhinoceros beetle can carry more than eight hundred times its own bodyweight. That is equivalent to you or me lifting up a tank!

- The fastest insect that we know of is the horsefly – one has been measured zipping around at 90 miles per hour!

- The longest insect so far discovered of is *phobaeticus chani* – a species of stick insect. An example kept in London's Natural History museum was 57cm in length!

- The most venomous insect we know of is the harvester ant. Think of the difference in size between an ant and a rat. Now consider that *just three stings* from this ant would kill that rat!

- The longest-living insect is thought to be a termite – specifically a termite queen. They have been known to live for more than fifty years!

- The largest spider (by size) discovered to date is the giant huntsman spider, found in caves in Laos. Examples have been found with legspans of over 30 cm!
- The heaviest spider on the other hand is the Goliath Bird eating spider which can weigh more than 70 grams.

Beetles

- Beetles are the largest group of the 32 orders that insects are separated into.

- There are many different types of beetle, ranging from dull and drab to highly coloured ones such as the ladybirds (or ladybugs) which you will see in your garden.

- One of every four animals on earth is a beetle!

- A cockroach's brain is not in its head but in its body. If it happens to lose its head somehow, it can still live for nine days – but it will eventually die as it won't be able to eat!

- The longest beetle is the South American Longhorn Beetle, which is 25cm in length!

- The heaviest beetle is the African Goliath beetle, which weighs in at 100 grams!

- Most beetles have a kind of body armour – hard forewings which generally protect their more delicate flying wings.

- Beetles as an order have been around for around 230 million years – they even survived whatever it was that wiped out the dinosaurs!

- One species of beetle, the whirligig, swims on water and has eyes which are split halfway through. This means that they can see both above and below the surface at the same time!

- One beetle with a fantastic name is surely the devil's coach horse, which – when it is feeling threatened – raises the rear of its body up and opens its fierce jaws!

Did You Know?

- Only male crickets chirp.

- A flea can jump more than two hundred times its own height. This would be like a grown man leaping to the top of the empire state building from the ground!

- There are three types of animal on the planet which fight in battle formations – humans, crows and ants.

- The combined weight of all the insects in the world is twelve times greater than the weight of the entire human population. Think of that next time you pick a fight with one!

- Earwigs are so called because people once believed they would climb into someone's ear and burrow their way into the person's brain! Of course, we now know this not to be true!

- Fireflies aren't actually flies – they are beetles!

- A typical mattress is home to more than six billion dustmites!

- No two spider webs are the same.

- Mosquitos prefer to bite children rather than adults, and prefer blonde ones to brunettes – yet no-one knows why.

- Some species of bees and cockroaches hold votes on important decisions such as where to make their next home.

Spiders

- Spiders have two body parts – a head and an abdomen.

- The diving bell spider lives its life underwater, and breathes by making a bubble full of air at the surface, then living inside it!

- A given weight of spider silk is around five times as strong as the same weight of steel.

- Tarantulas can survive for two whole years without food.

- Most spiders have either six or eight eyes.

- They also have fangs, which they use to bite their prey, injecting venom into it.

- Spiders eat many harmful insects in your garden, and are actually great at keeping it free of pests!

- Spiders are usually very short sighted, so use the hairs on their body to detect movement in the area.

- The tip of a spider's abdomen is home to glands known as *spinnerets* – from where the spiders make their silk. However, not all spiders spin webs.

- Many species of spider roll their old web up into a ball, eat it and spin a new web every day!

- More amazing facts about spiders can be found later on in this book!

Unusual Arthropods

- The praying mantis can swivel its head by 180 degrees to search for its prey.

- African termite mounds can be over twelve metres high.

- The mounds have a complicated network of vents which means they act as ventilation shafts which regulate the temperature of the nest. This ensures optimum conditions in which the termite queen can reproduce.

- Mosquitos have killed more humans than every war in history, ever!

- Some grasshoppers have ears on their legs.

- It is thought by some scientists that millipedes were the first animals to make their way out of the water to the land and breathe air. Fossils of millipedes (or at least their close ancestors) have been found that are more than four hundred million years old.

- Woodlice are common land-based crustaceans, and are unusual in that they are known by many different names. People across the world call them things such as armadillo bugs, cheeselogs, doodlebugs, sow bugs, chucky pigs and butcher boys.

- The stink bug is so called because when threatened it releases a disgusting odour – of course this would *usually* put off a predator who was intending to eat it!

- The largest butterfly in the world is the *queen Alexandra's birdwing*, the females of which can have a wingspan of more than 30 cm.
- Dragonflies have a life span of just one single day.

Amazing Ants

- Scientist believe that ants evolved around 130 million years ago, when dinosaurs still roamed the earth!

- There are more than twelve thousand species of ant in the world.

- For every human on this planet, there are one million ants.

- Ants 'hear' by feeling vibrations of the ground through their feet.

- Compared to their size, ants have much thicker muscles than humans. This enables some species of ant to lift over fifty times their bodyweight with their mandibles!

- The soldiers of some species of ant have developed their heads into the exact same shape as the entrance to their nests – which they guard by sitting inside with their heads stuck into the opening like a cork in a bottle!

- Some ants actually herd aphids. They carry them from plant to plant, encouraging them to feed so they can take advantage of the sugary sap they excrete.

- Some male driver ants (a species of army ant) are more than five centimetres long!

- When a scout ant discovers a source of food, it will lay a scent trail for other ants to follow so they can take the food back to their nests.

- If the queen of an ant colony dies, usually the colony dies too – it is rather rare for a queen to be replaced, and only she can reproduce.

Scorpions

- There are around 1500 species of Scorpion on the planet.

- Scorpions are easily recognisable because of their large front claws, and thin, segmented tail.

- All scorpions have venomous tails, and use these to kill their food and to defend themselves from other predators.

- Around twenty-five species of scorpion are venomous enough to kill a human.

- They are particularly fond of tight spaces where they feel protected – this is why they often hide in people's shoes when they find their way into houses!

- Shockingly, some female scorpions kill their male partners after they have mated.

- Even worse, if a mother scorpion is hungry after giving birth, sometimes she just eats her offspring!

- If this thankfully (for the young, at least!) doesn't happen, the baby scorpions will ride around on their mother's back for the first few weeks of their lives.

- Scorpions have between six and twelve eyes – but despite this have very poor vision!

- To make up for the poor eyesight, they have an excellent sense of smell which allows them to seek out food.

The Most Amazing Facts

- There are types of moth, called *Lachryphagous* moths, which live of the tears of horses, buffalo and other animals.

- Horrifically, a female praying mantis will kill its male partner, snapping its body in two and eating its head *whilst the two are actually mating!*

- The egg of the *Malaysian giant stick insect* is just 4mm wide, but when a baby hatches, it can already be more than 5 cm in length!

- Some ants, such as *Amazon ants*, have been known to invade colonies of other species of ant, kill the queen and enslave the enemy workers to do their bidding.

- The world's most poisonous spider is said to be the *Brazilian wandering spider*, the venom of which contains a highly potent neurotoxin.

- *Deathwatch* beetles make a very loud noise by banging their heads against the wooden walls of their tunnels!

- Some scorpions have an incredible ability which allows them to slow their metabolism right down, enabling them to survive when times are tough. Some have been known to survive on just a single meal a year, whilst others (in perhaps rather cruel experiments) have been frozen overnight only to thaw out the next day and walk away as if nothing has happened!

- *Indian moon moths* can smell a mate from an incredible six miles away.
- Some wasps sleep whilst they are hanging by their teeth!
- A housefly can taste with its feet, which are many orders of magnitude more sensitive than your tongue!

And Finally...

- Scientists have found out how to interpret the dance that one honey bee uses to communicate the location of a source of food to others. Amazingly, they have found that even if a bee didn't fly the direct route it communicates, it will work out all of the angles in its head and give the other bees the most efficient route. It even considers the curvature of the earth whilst making these calculations.

101 Amazing Facts about Sharks

The Basics

- Sharks are a type of fish which have certain characteristics including pectoral fins that are not fused to the head, between five and seven gill slits and a skeleton made from cartilage.

- There are over five hundred species of sharks living in the planet's oceans.

- Sharks are found in almost every sea on the planet.

- The method by which a shark swims can be compared to that of how an airplane flies; as it swishes its tail to move itself forwards (like a propeller), water moves over its fins which creates a kind of lift, like a plane's wings.

- Sharks can swim hundreds of miles in just a single day.

- Signs that a shark is about to attack its prey include a hunching of the back, a lowering of its pectoral fins and swimming in a zig-zag pattern.

- Sharks can dislocate their upper jaws to help them grab and hold onto their prey.

- Rather than scales, sharks have a special type of skin called *denticles* which allow them to move swiftly through the water without picking up barnacles and suchlike.

- The average shark lives to around the age of 25, however some can survive for over one hundred years.

- Many sharks are excellent hunters, stalking their prey from a distance until the perfect moment arises for them to strike.

A Great White Shark

General Facts

- Some great white sharks have been observed jumping up to three metres out of the water to catch nearby seals.

- Some sharks eat their siblings whilst they are still in their mother's womb – this isn't because they are 'naturally evil', it just happens to be the best source of nutrients as they are growing!

- Injured and dying fish often make a sound that is too low for humans to hear but that sharks have a keen perception for. Scientists have dubbed this noise the 'yummy hum'!

- At the back of each of its eyes, a shark has a membrane called the *tapetum lucidum* which reflects as much light as possible back into the eye itself. This therefore means that the shark can see in murky water or low-light conditions much better than animals without this ability.

- More people are killed every year by falling coconuts than they are by sharks.

- The *cookie cutter shark* fools its prey into thinking it is a small snack! The shark has a small strip on its neck that is designed to look like a much smaller fish, which the unwary enemy may fancy as a light snack. As it approaches closer however, the cookie cutter quickly takes a bite out of its would-be attacker and swims away!

- A species called the *gill frilled shark* was discovered off the coast of Japan in 2007. This incredible creature is closer in evolutionary terms to the sharks of prehistoric times and has certainly made many marine biologists wonder what else may be swimming undiscovered in the world's oceans!

- Sharks have many different senses to humans. For instance, they are able to sense pressure waves in the water through their lateral line organs, enabling them to detect the location of a target, and even the direction in which it is swimming.

- Some species of shark have organs called *photospheres* which emit light; we believe this is either to act as a kind of camouflage or to attract a mate.

- The reason that hammerhead sharks have such an unusual shape is that they have electroreceptors along their particularly wide heads which allow them to pinpoint potential prey better and thus become even more efficient hunters.

Shark Attacks

- Only three per cent of the world's shark species are known to attack humans.

- Shark attacks on humans are rare, however they *do* happen – there are around forty or fifty reports of this every year.

- Although many people are afraid of sharks, it is *they* who should be scared of *us*; humans kill around eighty million of them every year.

- Many people are scared of being attacked and killed by a shark, however the chances of this happening are much lower than being killed by dogs, bees or wasps.

- It is in fact even rarer that an attack is fatal; only between one tenth and one fifth of all shark attacks on humans result in death.

- The three most likely species of shark to attack humans are the *great white*, the *tiger shark* and the *bull shark*. The main reasons for this is that their prey is usually human sized, and they are top of the food chain so aren't scared of anything – including us!

- If a shark *does* bite a human, it usually *won't* have a second try. Once it has figured out the flesh it has ripped off is not from a sea creature (as we taste very different to them) it will usually swim away.

- The region that has seen the most shark attacks is Volusia County; there have been more than two hundred attacks here since the late 1800s – although most of them were minor bites rather than fatalities.

- The majority of people when asked would say that the shark they were most afraid of would be the great white. Yet between 1580 and 2007 – a period of over four hundred years – there has only been a total of 64 fatal attacks by the species.

- Somewhat amusingly, the chances of being bitten by a shark is significantly lower than being bitten by another human being!

A Bull Shark

Shark Biology

- A shark's liver contains a large amount of oil, which acts as a buoyancy aid and keeps it balanced in the water.

- Some (but not all) sharks need to keep moving otherwise they will drown. Species such as the great white and the mako do not have muscles that pump water through their mouths and over their gills; they need the flow of the water as they are swimming to do this.

- It is not the look of blood in the water that attracts a shark; it is in fact another sense altogether. Sharks have electroreceptors that can detect even the smallest change in an underwater environment. As blood alters the water's conductivity, it is actually *this* that alerts a shark to the situation.

- Most sharks have an excellent sense of hearing. This, and the fact that sound waves travel better through the water than they do through the air, means that they can hear potential prey swimming from many miles away.

- Whereas an average human being eats around half a ton of food every year, the average great white shark eats closer to eleven tons!

- Some sharks are born live, whereas others hatch from eggs. These are often known as 'mermaid's purses'; they are tough and leathery, very unlike the eggs of a chicken for instance.

- Sharks have rows and rows of teeth, but these aren't used for chewing; they are there to rip off huge chunks of flesh which are then swallowed whole.

- The usual gestation period of a shark is between six months and two years, depending on the species.

- Sharks have a field of vision which spans almost three hundred and sixty degrees. They generally only have two blind spots – one right in front of their nose and another just behind their head.

- Up to eighty per cent of a shark's flesh is in fact made up of water.

Various Shark Species

- The *whale shark* can live up to one hundred years, and doesn't reproduce until it is at least thirty years old.

- Although whale sharks are huge, they are pretty docile creatures – in fact they are not even meat eaters! These sharks are known as 'filter feeders' and actually use their rows of teeth to gather plankton.

- The natural habitat for *bull sharks* is the ocean, however they have often been seen in bays or lagoons and have even been known to swim up-river, sometimes even hundreds of miles inland.

- The *tiger shark* has not one but two wombs which means that is almost always gives birth to two pups.

- The *blue shark* has litters of pups numbering up to one hundred. Due to their tendency to swim in schools segregated by their sex and size, they are often known as 'the wolves of the sea'.

- Blue sharks just don't know when to stop eating. In fact, they carry on until they vomit out what they have swallowed... and then start eating again!

- In 1976 scientists discovered an unusual-looking species which has huge jaws extending in front of its eyes – yet despite its grim appearance is actually a filter feeder like the whale shark. This species is known as the *megamouth*.

- The *great hammerhead* has been known to swim from the coast of Florida all the way to the polar regions.

- One species we know very little about is the *goblin shark*. These strange looking creatures live in underwater mountain ranges so deep that it is almost impossible for us to study them.

- The *angel shark* buries itself in a pile of sand, lying in wait until suitable prey swims over... at which point it will quickly attack. This behaviour has led the species to be known as 'sand devils'.

A Whale Shark

Did You Know?

- You can often find shark's teeth that have fallen out and washed up on the beach. Sediments in the sand turn the teeth from their original clear white colour to a more faded grey or brown.

- The fear of sharks is known as *galeophobia*; the word comes from *galeos,* the ancient Greek word for a particular species of shark.

- Smaller sharks tend to feed near the ocean floor, whereas larger species roam higher – often at the surface, where larger prey such as seals can be found swimming.

- It is thought that the movie *Jaws* contributed to a statistically significant drop in the number of people visiting America's beaches during the late 1970s!

- It was also only after *Jaws* was made that recreational shark fishing (which has led to a tragic decline in population numbers) became popular, with many people wanting to experience the 'thrill' of catching a 'man-eating' great white.

- One potential environmentally safe way of warding off sharks is through magnets, which appear to confuse the shark's electro receptors.

- The moon's pull on the oceans can affect the feeding habits of sharks quite significantly, at extremes of its phase even drawing them much closer to the shore than normal.

- A shark can exert a pressure of up to forty thousand pounds per square inch with its bite.

- In 1978 archaeologists discovered the remains of the bodies of sharks in the ruins of the Aztec great temple; it is thought that they were used as a sacrifice to the gods.

- Although sharks are generally at the top of the food chain, there are some animals which have been known to eat them. These include seals, killer whales and crocodiles – and sometimes, even larger sharks!

A Great White Shark

Records

- The world's biggest shark is the whale shark. Adults of the species regularly clock in at ten metres long, and the largest measured was 12.65 metres. Many seafarers and divers do claim to have seen even larger examples – some even fifteen metres in length!

- The largest tiger shark ever caught weighed an amazing 1780 pounds and was captured in 1964 off the coast of South Carolina.

- The biggest thresher shark ever to have been caught weighed in at 1250 pounds and was captured off the coast of Cornwall in the UK.

- The largest Mako shark ever caught to date weighed in at 805 pounds and was captured off the coast of Florida.

- The largest shark ever to have lived is thought to be *Megalodon*. This brute which lived in prehistoric times is thought to have grown up to twenty metres long!

- The smallest shark we know of is the *dwarf lanternshark*, which only grows to around 17 centimetres in length.

- The longest great white shark ever caught was an incredible twelve and a half metres long and was captured off the coast of the Azores islands by a Portuguese fishing trawler.

- Experts believe that the rarest shark that we know of is the megamouth shark.

- the *shortfin mako shark* is believed to be the fastest species. They have been measured at speeds of more than thirty miles per hour, and it is thought they can reach speeds of up to fifty miles per hour!
- The *sawshark* has the longest nose of any species of shark; they use their flat nose (which is surrounded by blades like you would find on a saw) to swipe sideways at prey.

A Hammerhead Shark

Myths about Sharks

- Although many people believe it, it is *not* true that sharks don't attack in the middle of the day. This belief may have come about because there are less people in the water at lunchtime (as they have usually come out to rest or eat) and therefore statistically fewer attacks happen at this time – however this has nothing to do with shark behaviour and all to do with that of us humans!

- It certainly isn't true that the great white will eat *anything*. In fact, they are exceedingly picky eaters. To remain healthy, a great white needs a high fat content in its diet, and therefore will swim away after one bite if it doesn't think its current target will suit its dietary needs.

- Tiger sharks on the other hand are a little different. Scientists have discovered a wide range of objects inside caught specimens including tyres, license plates and even gasoline tanks!

- Some people think that sharks have to turn on their side to bite – this is completely untrue; they can bite from any angle!

- It has been said that one can stare down a shark as a line of defence. Amazingly, this is actually true. The advice given is that if you find yourself in a confrontation with a shark and have no means of escape, a good strategy is to look the fish straight in the eye, swim towards it, wave your arms about and scream.

- People say that if you are attacked by a shark, punching it in the nose will put it off. This isn't true – it is better to aim for the gills, as this is a much more sensitive area and will likely result in the shark swimming off to find easier prey.

- It is said that sharks don't get cancer; this is despite scientists knowing (and having proven) that this simply isn't true as long ago as the nineteenth century!

- It is not true that sharks are colour blind. Scientists believe that some sharks are attracted to certain colours, for instance the bright yellow which features on some divers' wetsuits!

- Some people believe that eating shark cartilage pills help fight cancer – this isn't true, and can actually make you very sick indeed. However it should be said that researchers *do* believe there may be some benefit to humans from the molecules that make up shark cartilage and *are* looking into scientific ways that we can learn from them.

- The Aztecs believed that attaching a string of chili peppers to their boats would ward off sharks, although scientists today do not believe this would have been an effective deterrent.

Conservation

- The World Conservation Union believes that almost thirty per cent of the world's species of shark are close to extinction due (in the main) to commercial fishing boats accidentally catching them in their nets.

- Overfishing has led to the numbers of some species of shark dwindling to 10% of what they were just one hundred years ago.

- The population of sharks in the Mediterranean sea has declined by an astounding 97 per cent in just two hundred years.

- Some conservationists risk their lives by diving underwater to free sharks that are trapped in fishing nets intended for other species.

- There are two main types of tracking device that are often used to learn more about sharks in the wild. One type is called SPOT and stands for 'Smart Position-Only Tag'; this device records information about the shark's location and transmits it to a satellite. The other is PAT, which stands for 'Pop-Up Archival Tag'; this records the information on the device itself, removing itself from the shark (and 'popping up' through the water) at a specified time.

- Due to the US government's protection of sea lions, seals, sea otters and other animals off the coast of California, there has been an increase of the shark population in the same area – because, of course, these creatures form a key part of the diet of some large species.

- Shark fin soup is considered a delicacy in much of China, and leads to the death of millions of sharks every year – enough even to raise concerns of extinction. Many are caught, have their fins cut off and then thrown back into the ocean to die a slow and painful death. Even more tragically, the practice is completely pointless even for culinary reasons – shark fins have almost no taste.

- Shockingly, the US Fishing industry also exports over two hundred thousand kilograms of shark fins to Hong Kong every single year.

- Spain is the country that exports the highest amount of shark fins; in 2008 they sold over *two and a half million kilograms* to Hong Kong.

- There are many charities that have been set up to assist with the conservation of sharks that you may wish to donate to. One in particular is the Shark Trust (UK) who can be found at www.sharktrust.co.uk

The Most Amazing Facts

- The film *Jaws* is in amazingly based on a real-life incident when four people were attacked by a shark off the coast of New Jersey in 1916!

- Some female sharks take sperm from a number of different males in one mating period, meaning that one litter can consist of pups who are 'half-brothers' – they have the same mother but different fathers!

- Scientists believe that one reason surfers may be attacked by sharks (and in particular by the great white) is that the outline of a person paddling through the water on a surfboard can look confusingly like that of a seal or turtle – very much a 'normal' meal for them.

- Very occasionally, it has been observed that female sharks have reproduced without any input from a male of the species; this act is known as parthenogenesis.

- As mentioned previously, there are a number of species of shark which have to keep swimming to ensure that enough water (and therefore oxygen) flows through their gills to keep them alive. The reef shark is one of these species, however – amazingly – scientists found a place in the ocean near Mexico where high levels of oxygen and low levels of salt allowed a huge number of reef sharks to lie motionless. Beautifully, this place is called the *Cave of Sleeping Sharks*.

- The great white shark does not have eyelids. When it attacks, in order to prevent its eyes from receiving damage from its prey thrashing about, it rolls them back into its head!

- The worst shark attack (on humans) in history is believed to have occurred during the second world war, when the USS Indianapolis was sunk in the Philippine sea near Guam. Around nine hundred sailors were stranded in the water, yet when rescuers reached them only three hundred and sixteen men were still alive – the majority are believed to have been eaten by sharks.

- A shark's electroreceptors are situated in nodules on their noses which are called *ampullae of Lorenzini*. The receptors can sense the direction that any electrical field is coming from. Ingeniously, this means that even the tiniest fluctuation that comes from an animal's beating heart can be picked up – so much so that it can act like a 'homing beacon' to the hungry shark!

- Shark's skeletons are made completely of a soft, elastic tissue called cartilage which is very different to bone. When a shark dies, its skin, organs, flesh and skeleton are entirely dissolved by the salt in the ocean, and the only thing that is left is its teeth.

- When in a feeding frenzy, there are still rules amongst sharks. For instance, Caribbean reef sharks have a clear 'pecking order' in which the largest sharks get to feed first!

And Finally...

▶ Sharks have lived on this planet for an extraordinary amount of time. We now believe they evolved over 400 million years ago; amazingly that is before even the dinosaurs roamed the planet!

A Hammerhead Shark

101 Amazing Facts about Cats

General Facts – Part 1

- A cat can't move its jaws sideways like you can.
- A group of kittens is called a *kindle*...
- ...Whereas a group of adult cats is called a *clowder*.
- A cat's heart beats twice as fast as a human's.
- The most popular names given to cats in America are *Samantha* and *Tiger*.
- Cats can determine if someone in a room has an animal hair allergy. No-one knows why, but they will try to sit on that person's lap first – really!
- Despite the phrase about grinning (and the character in *Alice in Wonderland*) there is no such breed as a Cheshire Cat. It is thought that the saying relates to the shape of the mould for Cheshire cheese, which looked like a smiling cat.
- In most countries, a black cat crossing your path is considered to be bad luck – however in Scotland they say it is a sign of upcoming good fortune.
- Weirdly, Medieval people in France and England believed that a black cat crossing your path in moonlight was a sign you would die in a horrible epidemic of disease.
- The most popular breed of cat is the Persian.

Statistics

- There are more than five hundred million cats in the world.
- There are around one hundred different breeds of domestic cat.
- 30% of a cat's waking hours are spent grooming themselves.
- Over its life, the average cat purrs for more than ten thousand hours.
- The heaviest cat ever recorded weighed nearly fifty pounds.
- On average, cats sleep for around sixteen hours a day.
- An average cat can run at a speed of 30 miles per hour.
- A cat can jump around five times its own height.
- Around seven percent of cats snore.
- The oldest cat to give birth was thirty years old – she had a small litter of just two kittens.

Unusual Facts

- Cat urine will glow underneath a black light – this helps find the location if you think your kitten has had an accident in the house!
- If you talk to your cat more, it will 'talk' back to you more!
- Most cats don't have any eyelashes.
- Killing a cat was a crime that carried the death penalty in ancient Egypt.
- In English, we say that cats go 'meow', but in Japan they say that they go 'nyaa'.
- In Ancient Egypt however, they said the noise was 'Mau' – and this is also the word they used for cat!
- Horrifyingly, when people in England were put to death for witchcraft, their cats were often put to death as well. Awful.
- Cats can't taste sweets.
- Napoleon, the Emperor of France, was terrified of cats.
- Cats don't knock things over by accident – animal behaviouralists think that they are either doing it for fun or to attract your attention... they are smart, aren't they!

Biology

- Most cats have four toes on each back foot, but five toes on each of their front feet!

- Some people will tell you cats are colorblind – but this is not true! Cats can definitely see reds, blues and greens.

- The oldest cat on record was called Puss. She lived to be an amazing 36 years old.

- Cats have four rows of whiskers.

- The largest domestic cat breed is generally considered to be the Maine Coon cat.

- Sadly, many white cats with blue eyes are deaf when they are born.

- A cat's field of vision is 220 degrees, whereas a human's is just 180.

- Cats have 24 more bones in their body than humans do.

- When a cat drinks, it is actually lapping up water from the underside of its tongue, not the top!

- A cat uses its whiskers to tell whether a gap is large enough for it to fit through.

Wildcats and Big Cats

- One difference between domesticated and wild cats is that domesticated breeds hold their tails straight up whilst walking; wild cats hold it either between their legs or horizontally.

- The Scottish wildcat is Britain's only remaining large wild predator.

- The largest wildcat is the Siberian tiger, which can grow to nearly 4 metres in length.

- The smallest on the other hand is the black-footed cat, which is just 50cm long.

- There are a number of famous 'beasts' across the world that are thought to be big cats that have escaped from captivity. Perhaps the most famous in Europe is the 'Beast of Bodmin Moor' which some think is an escaped puma.

- The cheetah is the world's fastest mammal – they can run at speeds in excess of 70 miles per hour.

- No two tigers have the same pattern of stripes.

- You can hear a lion's roar over five miles away.

- Lions are the only cats that like to live in large groups (called prides).

- Some breeders are mating domestic cats with wildcats to give hybrid breeds (an example of this is the savannah cat). Whilst they may look incredible, they are expensive – and *very* hard to care for!

Kittens

- During a female cat's life, she can have more than one hundred kittens.

- A litter of kittens do not necessarily all come from the same father.

- The record for a 100% surviving litter was 14 kittens – the mother's name was Bluebell and she was a Persian cat.

- Kittens are born with a full set of teeth that fall out and get replaces just like a human's!

- Your kitten needs sleep to help it get bigger – its growth hormones are only released whilst it is asleep!

- Kittens hate dirty litter boxes and will often refuse to use them.

- When a kitten is first born, its heart beats around 250 times a minute.

- Most kittens are born with blue eyes – it is only when they are exposed to light that they change colour!

- It has been proven that kittens *do* dream when they're asleep.

- Important advice – don't feed your kitten grapes or raisins – they can cause kidney failure.

Behaviour

- Cats paw at the floor to mark their territory – they sweat through the bottom of their paws (and the sweat contains scent) which they rub on the ground.
- When a cat is near you and its tail lightly quivers, this is a sign of absolute love and affection.
- However if the tail is thrashing, it is in a very bad mood!
- Another sign of happiness is when a cat squeezes its eyes shut.
- Cats can be trained to use a human toilet instead of a litter box. Amazingly, some owners have even managed to train their cats to flush after going!
- When your cat brings you a dead mouse or bird, it isn't necessarily bringing you a present. Some animal behaviouralists believe that the cat thinks you are in fact a poor hunter, and is bringing you its prey because it thinks you are incapable of capturing it yourself!
- Scientists say that cats don't think of themselves as small humans – they think of humans as large cats!
- If your cat is frightened, covering its eyes helps it to calm down.
- If your cat rolls over onto its back and exposes its belly to you, it means that you are trusted!
- When your cat licks you it is a sign of affection.

Cats are Great!

- Cats can make ten times more vocal sounds than dogs can.

- Cats have the largest eyes in relation to their body size of any animal.

- A human's brain is more similar to a cat's than a dog's in the way it works.

- Sailors often bought cats as ship's mascots during both world wars. They were used to protect food supplies from mice, and were commonly given their own hammocks to sleep in!

- A cat can recognise its owner's unique footsteps from up to one hundred metres away.

- Your cat's tongue is covered in many tiny hooks which help in tearing food apart in its mouth.

- A cat can turn to the direction of a sound it hears ten times faster than the best watchdog.

- Hearing is a real strong-point – your cat can rotate each ear independently and with a range of 180 degrees.

- Americans own 73 million cats whereas they only own 63 million dogs, meaning cats win the USA popularity contest!

- Cats do not have a collarbone, meaning they can fit through almost any opening smaller than their head!

General Facts – Part 2

- When a cat nips at you during petting, it is their way of telling you they are enjoying the attention.

- Female cats mature quicker than male ones – they can reach adulthood in just five months, whereas males can take almost twice as long.

- Cats eat grass so they can regurgitate hair and other irritants, ensuring their digestive system stay clean.

- Most cats are actually lactose intolerant, so drinking milk gives them a stomach-ache and diarrhoea.

- Scientists think that cats respond better to women because their voices are higher pitched.

- The biological name for a cat's hairball is a *bezoar*.

- The first cat in space was from France and was called Felicette. You'll be pleased to know that she survived the trip.

- In the original version of *Cinderella* (which was told in Italy), the fairy godmother was actually a cat.

- Cats generally only meow at humans – they rarely make the noise to other cats!

- The first cat show (in modern times) was held in London in 1871.

The Most Amazing Facts

- A cat's nose has a unique pattern – just like the human fingerprint!

- Who invented the cat flap? Amazingly, it was the man who discovered the principles of gravity, Isaac Newton!

- Americans spend more on cat food every year than they do on baby food!

- In 1879, the Belgian Post Office tried to use 37 cats to deliver the mail. It worked for a while, but the cats weren't disciplined enough to keep it up!

- People often wonder why there is not mouse-flavored cat food. This is because cat food companies have tried to make it, but in tests cats didn't actually like it!

- Ancient Egyptians worshipped cats. If a cat died, the family who 'owned' the cat would shave off their eyebrows as a sign of mourning.

- If you suffer from high blood pressure, you should get a cat – it has been proven that stroking a cat helps lower it!

- Studies have shown that cats respond most readily to names that end with an 'ee' sound!

- A cat called Towser worked at the Glenturret Distillery in Scotland and caught nearly thirty thousand mice in twenty-four years. When she sadly died, she was replaced by a cat called Amber. Amber never caught a single mouse.

- During the second world war, a cat was awarded the Dickin Medal for Bravery – this is the animal version of the Victoria Cross!

And Finally...

- In the Dutch embassy in Moscow, staff noticed two cats kept as pets in the building kept clawing at a particular wall. When they investigated further – and thinking they would find mice – there were actually microphones hidden there by Russian spies!

101 Amazing Facts about Birds

General Facts

- The characteristics of birds are that they have feathers, wings, are warm-blooded and lay eggs.

- More than ten thousand species of bird are believed to exist across the planet.

- Birds have special lightweight skeletons which enable them to fly – many of their bones are actually hollow.

- The most intelligent birds across the world have been seen using tools to complete tasks in the wild – something which scientists of previous generations did not think possible.

- It is thought that birds today are direct descendants of the dinosaurs.

- When migratory birds fly their long journeys, they often do so in a 'V' formation – this has been proven to reduce drag and therefore use less energy throughout the trip.

- The shape of a bird's beak depends on what its diet in the wild consists of.

- Some birds, such as the kingfisher, the swift and the grebe cannot actually walk.

- Generally, birds walk on their toes with their heels in the air.

- The plumage of male and female birds often varies greatly; most of the time it is the male of the species with the more 'showy' colours.

Collective Nouns – Part 1

Here are some of the more unusual collective nouns for birds...

- A *siege* of bitterns.

- A *bellowing* of bullfinches.

- A *gulp* of cormorants.

- A *murder* of crows.

- A *wake* of buzzards.

- A *piteousness* of doves.

- A *congress* of eagles.

- A *bazaar* of guillemots.

- A *clattering* of jackdaws.

- A *parliament* of rooks.

Record Breakers – Part 1

- The peregrine falcon has been known to dive at speeds of more than 240 miles per hour, making it the fastest recorded bird on the planet.

- For *powered* flight though, the spine-tailed swift is the fastest, at 106 miles per hour.

- The longest feathers ever measured were on a Japanese phoenix fowl – its tail feathers were over ten metres long!

- The Australian pelican has the longest beak of any bird – it is half a metre in length!

- The wandering albatross has the greatest wingspan of any bird – over three and a half metres.

- The bee hummingbird is the smallest bird in the world – it is just 7 cm long and weighs only one and a half grams. Amazingly, its beak and tail make up half of its tiny length!

- Gentoo penguins hold the record for the fastest swimming bird – twenty-five miles per hour!

- The tallest bird which can fly is the crane – some have been known to stand two metres high!

- The heaviest flying bird is the great bustard, which can weigh as much as 21 kilograms.

- The kiwi lays the largest egg relative to its body size of any bird in the world.

Parrots

- There are more than 350 different species of parrot.

- At the time of writing, Poncho the parrot is thought to be the oldest ever member of her species, having celebrated her 87th birthday in 2012. Despite her age, she has starred in films such as *Ace Ventura* and *102 Dalmatians*.

- The largest species of parrot is the hyacinth macaw, which can grow to over one metre long.

- The smallest on the other hand are the New Guinea pygmy parrots, with adults only reaching 8 cm in length.

- Most parrots don't build nests, although one exception to the rule is the quaker parrot – they actually build nests which link to one another, forming colony habitations.

- In the wild, parrots can fly as much as 500 miles in just one day to look for food.

- It is thought by many scientists that talking parrots are not just mimicking what they hear, but can also display an understanding of speech – some think they have the same mental prowess as a two year old!

- Like parrots, the toucan can be taught a number of words and phrases.

- A Parrot is actually featured on the flag of Dominica – the bird chosen is the Sisserou parrot and is native to the island.

- Alex the parrot was an African grey owned by animal psychologist Irene Pepperberg. He had a vocabulary of over one hundred words, and also showed that he *understood* them. Sadly, he died unexpectedly overnight; his last words to Irene before she went to bed were "You be good, see you tomorrow. I love you."

Interesting Facts

- After eating a rat whole, an owl will then vomit out a pellet containing its fur and bones.

- Flamingos are actually born grey, however they acquire their distinctive pink colour from a natural dye called canthaxanthin which is found in their diet of shrimp and algae.

- After leaving its nest, the swallow spends the first four years of its life in the air!

- A chicken egg was once cracked open that had nine different yolks in it!

- There is a genus of birds native to New Guinea called the pitohui; three species of pitohui have been found to be poisonous, and are the first birds ever to have been discovered that are so.

- The kiwi is the only known bird without wings.

- During the first world war, it was common to use homing pigeons to send messages. One, by the name of Cher Ami lost a leg whilst carrying an important message (due to enemy fire), but still found its way to its intended recipient. She was awarded with a distinguished service medal – and a wooden leg!

- The kelp gull is known to attack an animal far bigger than itself for food... flocks of them have been seen waiting for whales to surface, and them stab them with their strong beaks, ripping out large chunks of flesh and blubber.

- If a baby stork is not happy with the way it is being reared, it sometimes abandons its parents and wanders into another nearby nest to be fed by a new family!

- The tawny frogmouth is an unusual predator. It does not chase its prey, rather it camouflages itself on a tree with its beak wide open. Its disguise is so good that lizards, grubs and even other birds do not see it for what it is, and crawl into its mouth – which promptly snaps shut like a Venus flytrap, giving the frogmouth a lovely meal.

Record Breakers – Part 2

- The ostrich is the world's largest bird, and can weigh more than 140 kg.

- Also, ostriches not only have the biggest eyes of any bird, but amazingly they are also the largest of any land animal on the planet, measuring up to 5 cm in diameter.

- These amazing birds also hold a third world record – ostriches are the fastest running of all birds, and can achieve speeds of more than forty miles per hour!

- The turkey buzzard is the world's longest living bird, with one example reaching the grand old age of 118 years!

- The ruby-throated hummingbird holds the record for having the fastest wings, reaching 200 beats per second during mating season.

- There are more chickens than any other kind of bird in the world.

- The toucan has the biggest beak relative to its body size of any bird.

- The largest flying bird ever to have been discovered is the Argentavis, which lived around six million years ago. Its wingspan is thought to have been around seven metres, twice that of the largest bird today.

- The largest owl is the Eurasian Eagle owl, whose wingspan can reach one and a half metres. Despite this enormous size, they can fly silently by gliding – handy for catching their prey!

▶ The largest bird ever to have lived was the Madagascan elephant bird, which stood well over three metres tall, and weighed almost half a ton. Sadly it was hunted to extinction around four hundred years ago, and all we have left are skeletons of this magnificent species.

Collective Nouns – Part 2

Here are some more unusual collective nouns for birds...

- A *coil* of widgeon.

- A *mutation* of thrushes.

- A *phalanx* of storks.

- A *murmuration* of starlings.

- An *exaltation* of skylarks.

- A *prattle* of parrots.

- A *clattering* of jackdaws.

- A *troubling* of goldfinches.

- A *mews* of capons.

- A *raft* of auks.

Seabirds

- In its lifetime, an albatross is thought to fly around fifteen *million* miles! To put that into prespective, that is the same as flying halfway to Mars when the red planet and earth are at their closest. Incredible.

- The albatross uses a number of tricks to soar for hours without ever flapping its wings, thus saving a huge amount of energy. Some even sleep whilst they are flying!

- Seabirds have special salt glands near the base of their bills which filters salt from their bloodstream so that their kidneys don't become overloaded.

- In general, seabirds grow more slowly than land birds as they have to search for food over a wider area.

- Some seabirds such as petrels and albatrosses have specially enhanced senses of smell which allow them to find food over greater distances.

- Penguins have evolved so their feathers are more like scales and their wings are more like flippers. Although this prevents them from flying, it has meant they are much better suited to finding food in the sea.

- Every year the Arctic tern migrates from the Arctic to the Antarctic and back again – this is a distance of more than 20,000 miles.

- Emperor penguins can dive do an incredible depth of more than 240 metres – almost the height of the Trump Tower in New York!

- Cormorants have been trained to catch fish for humans in Asia for the last 1300 years – it is well worth watching a video of this amazing relationship online!
- Frigatebirds regularly chase other seabirds and make them vomit up their food... which they then eat!

IN MYTHOLOGY

- Athena, the Greek goddess of wisdom, was traditionally represented as having been accompanied by an owl. Because of this, owls are today seen as the symbol of knowledge throughout the Western world.

- The Norse god Odin was said to have two ravens – Huginn (thought) and Muninn (mind) – which flew all over the world, reported their findings back to him and also acted as his messengers.

- Crows and ravens have become associated with death. This may be because of their presence on battlefields of the past, where they would await the tasty morsels of flesh available at the end of the fighting!

- Doves are considered to symbolize hope; this association is referenced in many religions, including in the bible story of Noah.

- The roc was a huge white bird of prey in Arabic mythology, and was popularised in fairy tales from the region.

- The phoenix is perhaps the best known of mythological birds in the Western world; the Greeks believed it lived a cyclical life, whereby it would be consumed by fire at the end of its life, then reborn from its own ashes.

- Medieval Britons wrote extensively about the cockatrice – a dragon with the head of a rooster which could turn people to stone just by looking at them.

- In Greek mythology, the Harpy was a bird with the body of a vulture but the head of a woman. Originally the woman's face was a beautiful one, however by Roman times they were said to be hideous!
- The ziz is a bird in Jewish mythology, said to have wings so large that they could block out the sun.
- The thunderbird comes from Native American legends; it has the ability to create thunderstorms by flapping its wings and it is also considered to be a spiritual messenger which grants good fortune to those who dream of it.

Would You Believe?

- Woodpeckers tap the bark of a tree up to twenty times per second; they have evolved a sponge-like area behind their beak which acts as a kind of shock absorber.

- To give a hummingbird enough energy to flap its wings at an incredible 75 times per second, it needs to eat twice its bodyweight in nectar each and every day.

- Eagles have been known to kill and carry away prey as large as small deers!

- Ostriches can run faster than horses, and males of the species can emit a load roar!

- Flamingos can only eat when their heads are upside down.

- Some birds deliberately put ants into their feathers because the ants use their formic acid to kill parasites.

- Generally, a bird's feathers weigh more than its skeleton.

- When the hoopoe bird is attacked, it turns its body around and violently sprays its excrement at the approaching predator!

- The roadrunner bird has a rather horrible way of dealing with its young if they don't grow fast enough – it eats them!

- The humble wren can feed more than five hundred grubs and bugs to its young in just one day.

And Finally...

- Penguins expel their poop with force so it lands away from their nests. It goes so far that by comparison you would have to stand around two metres away from the toilet to achieve the same scale!

101 Amazing Facts about Horses

The Basics

- Horses were first domesticated around 5000 years ago.
- The domestic horse has a lifespan of around 25 years.
- Horses are herbivores.
- The speed of a galloping horse is around 27 miles per hour.
- It is thought that there are approximately seventy million horses in the world.
- The name for an adult male horse is *stallion*, with young males called *colts*.
- Adult female horses on the other hand are called *mares*, with young ones named *fillies*.
- All young horses regardless of sex are called *foals* for the first year of their life.
- The left side of a horse is its 'near side' and the right its 'off side'.
- Horses are measured in *hands* and *fingers* – one hand is set at four inches, and a finger is one inch. Therefore a horse which is 63 inches high is 15.3hh (fifteen hands and three fingers).

General Facts – Part 1

- In the wild, it is always a mare who decides when a herd moves on to graze in a new spot.

- Someone who makes and fits horseshoes is known as a *farrier*.

- There are four speeds your horse can travel at. From slowest to fastest they are *walk, trot, canter* and *gallop*.

- A marking on a horse's head is always referred to as a 'star' – even when it's not star-shaped!

- Horses can rotate their ears to place a sound better.

- The horse is one of the twelve signs of the Chinese Zodiac. If you are born in the year of the horse, you are said to be intelligent, independent and a free spirit.

- A horse will generally only sleep for between two and three hours per day.

- Horses' hooves are made from keratin, the same type of matter as fingernails and hair.

- The horse is the state animal of New Jersey.

- Horse meat is considered a delicacy in many countries across the world, especially in the great food-loving nation of France!

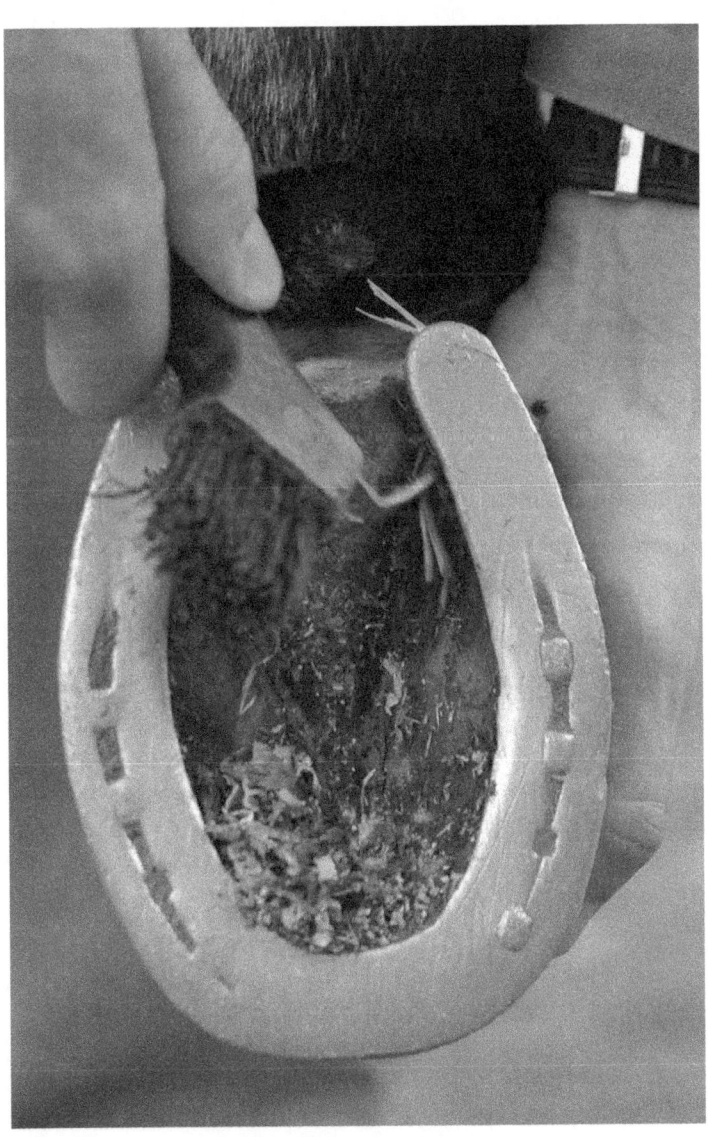

Cleaning a horse's hoof

Famous Horses

- **Secretariat** – an American Thoroughbred racehorse who set records in the Kentucky Derby, the Preakness Stakes and the Belmont Stakes which still stand today.

- **Man o'War** – sired in 1917 he won 20 out of 21 races and is considered to be one of the greatest Thoroughbred racehorses of all time.

- **Shergar** – winner of the 1981 Epsom Derby by ten lengths, a record still held today, he was stolen by masked gunmen in 1983 and was never seen again.

- **Red Rum** – his comeback in 1973 to win the Grand National from thirty lengths behind was voted the 24th greatest sporting moment of all time.

- **Mister Ed** – a palomino horse who appears to 'talk' in his classic American sitcom.

- **Black Beauty** – fictional star of Anna Sewell's famous novel.

- **Arkle** – Irish racehorse who was so good that the authorities had to invent a whole new weight system for races he was in – until that point other trainers didn't even bother to field horses in races in which Arkle was due to take part! Even when he carried two and a half stone more than any other horse in the 1964 Irish Grand National, he still won...

- **Frankel** – arguably the greatest racehorse of all time, winning every single one of the fourteen races he was entered in. At the end of his racing career he was valued at £100m ($165m)

- **Silver** – the Lone Ranger's horse. "Hi-Yo, Silver! Away!"
- **The Uffington White Horse** – huge chalk horse carved into the Berkshire Downs hillside 3000 years ago.

The Uffington White Horse

Record Breakers

- The oldest horse in history is reported to be 'Old Billy', a 19th century specimen who lived to the incredible age of 62!

- The fastest recorded speed a horse has reached is 55 miles per hour.

- The smallest mature horse in the world is called Einstein and he is just fourteen inches tall!

- At the date of writing, the most expensive horse sold at auction was The Green Monkey, which changed hands for $16m. He didn't turn out as expected though, only racing three times and coming no higher than third. He was retired two years later.

- The longest tail recorded on a horse is that of JJS Summer Breeze, which came in at an amazing 381cm!

- In 2009, an Italian stunt rider by the name of Gregory Ancelotti rode a horse called Doc 30 metres on its hind legs alone!

- The largest horse ever measured was called Brooklyn Supreme. He weighed 1500 kg and stood 19.2 hands tall – that's almost two metres!

- The world record for the highest observed jump made by a horse has stood for over sixty years. In 1949, Captain Alberto Larraguibel rode Huaso as he jumped a fence that was 8 feet and 1 inch high (247cm).

- A horse called 'Something' holds the record for the longest observed jump – in 1975 Andre Ferreira rode him whilst he jumped a distance of 8.4 metres.

- In 1983, Shareef Dancer became the most expensive horse ever sold privately. The price? An incredible $40m.

Alberto Larraguibel riding Huaso over the highest jump ever recorded

Different Breeds

- The Arabian horse has one less rib, one less lumbar bone and two fewer tail vertebrae than most other breeds.

- Although Camargue horses are a very light grey as adults, when they are born they are almost black! This is because not only is their skin black, but so is their coat at first. However as they reach maturity their hair grows lighter and lighter.

- The Shire Horse is generally thought to be the largest breed in the world; they are work horses and can pull extraordinary weights.

- A breed of horses called the Akhal-Teke from Turkmenistan can go for a number of days with no food or water.

- Mustangs are one of only a handful of breeds which live wild in the USA; they are closely related to the original breed that Spanish explorers brought to the country 400 years ago.

- The rarest breed is thought to be the Abaco Barb, a type of horse that only lives in the Bahamas. In a 2010 count, only five were found and the breed is likely to become extinct.

- The Shetland pony is generally considered to be the smallest horse breed, and evolved that way due to the harsh climate of the Shetland Isles in Scotland. It was first imported to the USA in 1885.

- Ponies are still horses; they are just generally smaller breeds – usually under 14.3 hands.
- All thoroughbred horses today can be traced back to just three sires: the Darley Arabian, the Byerley Turk and the Godolphin Arabian.
- The Anglo-Arab is a particularly brave an intelligent breed, and is used most often for dressage, eventing and jumping.

A Shire Horse at work

Medical Facts

- Horses have 205 bones.
- A horse's hoof grows around a quarter of an inch every month.
- A healthy horse's heart rate is around 38 beats per minute.
- Horses sleep for more hours in the summer than they do in the winter.
- A normal, healthy breathing rate for a mature horse is between eight and sixteen breaths per minute.
- Just like humans, horses have milk teeth; these are replaced by adult teeth between three and five years of age.
- Horses drink water in by sucking it up in a similar way to cattle, rather than the 'lapping' action of a cat or dog.
- A new-born foal can stand up within an hour of being born.
- Horses have a much better sense of smell than humans do!
- Male horses have more teeth than female ones!

A mare with her foal

Quotes about Horses

- "No heaven can heaven be, if my horse isn't there to welcome me."

- "When I bestride him, I soar, I am a hawk. He trots the air, the earth sings when he touches it." - *Shakespeare* (Henry V)

- "A dog may be man's best friend... but the horse wrote history."

- "A true horseman does not look at the horse with his eyes, he looks at his horse with his heart."

- "No philosophers so thoroughly comprehend us as dogs and horses." - *Herman Melville*

- "Ask me to show you poetry in motion and I will show you a horse."

- "No hour of life is wasted that is spent in the saddle." - *Winston Churchill*

- "To ride on a horse is to fly without wings."

- "Before I loved horses, I had nothing to live for. Now I love horses and can't stop seeing things to live for."

- "A pony is a childhood dream. A horse is an adulthood treasure." - *Rebecca Carroll*

A Shetland Pony

Did You Know?

- Horses can sleep whilst they are standing up.
- The offspring of a zebra and a donkey is called a *zedonk* whereas a cross between a horse and a zebra is called a *zebroid* or a *zorse*.
- Horses don't like the smell of pigs!
- Horses use their tales to tell each other how they are feeling.
- A horse is never said to be white (even when it looks it!) – the word used is always gray (or sometimes grey in the UK).
- Horses make different facial expressions to communicate their mood; they use their eyes, ears and nostrils for this purpose.
- The name of the soft, breathy whinny that mares usually make when nursing a foal is called a *whicker*.
- When a horse curls its lips back, this is called the *flehmen position*. The horse does this because it is 'sensing' the surroundings by drawing air into its vomeronasal organ.
- In the USA, the horse industry contributes around $120 billion to the economy – this is more than the movie industry!
- Horses are very social animals and get extremely lonely if they are kept alone.

A Zedonk

General Facts – Part 2

- In America, around two million people own horses.

- Thoroughbred horses are all given the same 'birthday' – the first of January. This makes it easier to calculate the ages of entrants for races.

- You can tell the age of a horse by looking at its teeth. A five year old horse will have all its teeth, and after that age they just grow longer.

- Horses' teeth fill up more space in their heads than their brains do!

- Horses only breathe through their noses, not through their mouths like we can.

- A hinny is a cross between a male horse and a female donkey, whereas a mule is a cross between a male donkey and a female horse. Both of these are generally sterile however there have been some exceptions in history.

- In 2010, the purse of the Dubai World Cup was raised to ten million dollars – this means it is the richest horse race in the world.

- An irrational fear of horses is called equinophobia.

- A horse's knee joint is similar to a human wrist, and their hock joint is a bit like a human ankle.

- The largest horse museum in the world is the *International Museum of the Horse* in Kentucky and is well worth a visit!

A Zebra demonstrating the flehmen position

The Most Amazing Facts

- During the first world war, around one million horses were used by the allied troops. Sadly, only 65,000 ever returned home.

- In a herd, one horse will always remain standing even if the others are lying down – this is because one is always chosen to act as a lookout for danger.

- There was not a single horse living in Australia until 1788.

- The first horse box (often called a horse trailer in America) was invented in Britain by Lord George Bentinck in 1836. Amazingly, it was pulled by six horses! This isn't as crazy as it sounds however, as he wanted a way of transporting his racehorses to meetings without tiring them out.

- Horses are completely unable to burp or vomit.

- The names Philip, Phillip and Phillipa come from the Greek Phillippos, a word which means 'lover of horses'.

- In 1872, a man called Leland Stanford placed a bet that during a horse's gallop, there is a point in time where all four legs are off the ground; everyone thought he was mad, as up until this point people assumed at least one foot was always touching the turf. However, Eadweard Muybridge set up a series of twenty-four cameras to photograph a racehorse called Sallie Gardner. As you might expect, the photographs proved Stanford correct!

- It is thought that the modern horse evolved from an animal called a hyracotherium which lived around 50 million years ago. The hyracotherium was the size of a small dog and had webbed feet!
- Horses have the largest eyes of any land mammal.
- When foals are born, their legs are already at 90% of their adult length!

Sallie Gardner in some of Eadweard Muybridge's photographs

And Finally...

- James Watt came up with the term 'horsepower' as he wanted to describe a measurement that people would be able to easily understand. One horsepower is the amount that a single horse can produce for a continuous time period at a slow haul. During a gallop however, one horse can produce almost fifteen horsepower!

A horse at a show jumping event

101 Amazing Facts about Snakes

The Basics

- Snakes are a legless reptiles belonging to a suborder with the Latin name *serpentes*.
- They are different to legless lizards that – unlike snakes – have eyelids and external ears.
- A common feature of all snakes is that their bodies are covered in overlapping scales.
- The suborder of serpentes is further separated into two types; these are *alethinophidia* and *scolecophidia*.
- The majority of snakes are alethinophidia, with the distinguishing characteristic of scolecophidia being that all species within the order are blind.
- There are fifteen 'families' of alethinophidia; these are file snakes, coral pipe snakes, dwarf pipe snakes, Asian pipe snakes, boas, dwarf boas, Round Island boas, colubrids, elapidae, shield-tailed & short-tailed snakes, sunbeam snakes, vipers (including pit vipers) & rattlesnakes, mole vipers, Mexican burrowing snakes and finally pythons.
- It is thought that there are over three thousand species of snake to be found on the planet.
- Snakes are found on every continent on earth except Antarctica.
- There are snakes inhabiting almost every large island on the planet; the two notable exceptions are New Zealand and Ireland.

- Most snakes are non-venomous, either swallowing their prey alive or squeezing it to death first; however there *are* some snakes whose venom is powerful enough to kill humans.

A Timber Rattlesnake

BIOLOGY

- Snakes are cold-blooded, which means you will generally find them in warm areas.

- The majority of snakes – around 70% – hatch from eggs. The rest in fact give birth to living young.

- The paired organs of snakes (such as their kidneys) are positioned in their bodies one behind the other, rather than side-by-side as they are in humans.

- Most snakes only have one lung.

- Generally snakes have very poor eyesight and rely on their other senses for everything from hunting and finding a mate to avoiding predators.

- Snakes *do* have ears, but amazingly they are inside their heads!

- It could be said that snakes 'smell' the air with their tongues; they have extremely sensitive receptors which can detect prey from a great distance.

- Some snakes are able to 'unlock' their jaws, enabling them to swallow prey that is much larger than their own heads.

- Snakes shed their skin multiple times every year; the process of doing this usually takes a few days.

- A snake's eyes will usually turn milky just before they shed their skin. This is because their eyes are also covered by scales that are shed – these are clear and called 'spectacle scales'.

An Indian Cobra

General Facts

- Snakes have a number of predators, including birds, mongooses, foxes, coyotes, boars and even other snakes.

- Those who keep snakes say that cobras are the most intelligent of all species, and can quickly learn to tell the difference between their owners and other people!

- The biggest threat to snakes today is humans; we kill them for their skin or out of fear, and we are responsible for destroying the habitats in which many of them live. Sadly there are many species that it is unlikely we will ever discover much about, as they will probably become extinct before we have had the chance to study them.

- Whereas some snakes leave their eggs after laying them, the female python will coil up around the eggs she has laid and vibrate her body to keep them warm until they hatch.

- The most common place to be bitten by a snake is of course on the leg – as this is usually the most exposed piece of your flesh that is close to the ground.

- In captivity, some species of snake can live over fifty years. We have found it difficult to determine how long snakes in the wild can live for, but it is thought that some species can live even longer than this.

- Biologically, snakes do in fact comprise of a head, body and tail – although it is generally difficult to determine where one part starts and another ends from just looking at a specimen.

- There are only four species of snake native to the United Kingdom; these are the Aesculapian snake, the smooth snake, the grass snake and the adder. Of these, only the adder – a type of viper – is poisonous, although attacks on humans are extremely rare.

- A snake's scales are made of *keratin* – the same material that makes up your hair and fingernails.

- It is thought that between twenty thousand and one hundred thousand people die every year from snake bites, with the majority of these happening in Asia and sub-Saharan Africa.

A Boa Constrictor

Interesting Species

- A species of sea-dwelling serpent called the *tentacle snake* is fascinating for two reasons. Firstly, it has two tentacles in front of its mouth which allow it to detect movement in the water. Secondly, it is the only known snake to anticipate the movement of its prey – it angles its head in a certain way prior to attacking, knowing that the fish on which it feeds will react by swimming in that direction.

- The *cantil snake* has a bright yellow tip on its tail that makes it look like a worm. This lures in potential prey, which the snake then lunges at when it is close enough.

- *Rattlesnakes* have rattles at the end of their tales which they shake to ward off predators. Although they generally hunt small animals such as mice and birds, they are known to commonly bite humans when threatened. The rattle is in fact made from around ten layers of scales that don't shed when the rest of its skin does.

- The *vine snake* is particularly notable for its unusually good sight, possessing binocular vision, unlike most other species.

- The unusual *atheris hispida*, also known as the *feathered tree viper* not only has an unusual appearance (with its bristle-like scales looking similar to the feathers of a bird) but also is one of the world's snakes for which we have not yet found an anti-venom.

- The *burrowing asp* has such long teeth that they protrude forwards when in use, meaning it can 'bite' even when its mouth is closed!

- The *corn snake* can angle its scales outwards to use as a kind of 'anchor'; this allows it to climb vertically up trees.

- The *Japanese water snake* 'steals' poison from venomous toads, storing it in a gland near its neck. When threatened it will release this venom in defence; this allows the individual to save its *own* venom for attacking prey.

- The *spitting cobra, hognose* and *grass snake* will all fake death when seriously threatened. They curl into an unusual position, lie on their backs and excrete an awful smelly substance from their anal opening!

- The *horned viper* usually has a pair of horns situated above its eyes; it also rubs against itself to produce a warning sound before it strikes – if you hear this you really need to back away quickly!

Did You Know?

- Almost all snakes are carnivorous; the only real exceptions are a few species that survive on a diet of eggs.

- The process of squeezing the breath out of prey to kill it is called *constriction*.

- Most snakes have teeth – usually four rows hanging from the top of their mouths and two extending from the bottom; however these teeth are for holding onto prey rather than chewing.

- Snakes have a small notch in their lips so they can stick out their tongues without opening their mouths!

- You can eat snake meat. It tastes like chicken, but is a little tougher.

- Only one species – the *king cobra* – builds a nest to protect its young. Until recently many people believed that all snakes did this.

- Unlike most other animals, a king cobra can effectively defend itself from predators from the moment that it is born.

- Snakes can 'hear' by sensing vibrations through the ground.

- Due to their low rate of metabolism, snakes can often go months without eating.

- Some snakes are called 'flying snakes' – although they don't actually fly, but can glide through the air after flinging themselves off high trees.

A Belcher Sea Snake

Venomous Snakes

- There are thought to be over seven hundred species of venomous snake.

- These snakes bite their prey, injecting venom into them through a duct in their teeth. The venom subdues the prey, making it easier to eat.

- Venomous snakes are very successful hunters. When they strike, they have almost a 100% success rate.

- Around one third of the venomous snake species can kill a human with just one bite.

- Cobras have an interesting defence mechanism; when threatened, they rise up and flatten their necks, making themselves appear larger.

- In North America, the species most commonly responsible for bites are rattlesnakes.

- If you do get bitten, you should get to a hospital straight away; scientists *have* now developed anti-venoms which 'cancel out' the effect of most snake bites.

- Some snakes have extremely long venomous fangs; these fold back into the snake's mouth so it doesn't bite itself!

- The most effective type of venom used by snakes is *neurotoxic*, which means it works by destroying the nervous system – this quickly stops any prey from breathing.

- Some of the *most* venomous snakes are in fact sea snakes – species that generally live underwater!

An Anaconda

Myths & Legends

- Many people think of snakes as 'slimy' but they couldn't be more wrong – snake skin is in fact dry.

- It is also not true that snakes hypnotize their prey, yet the myth is still widely believed cross the world.

- One Indian myth tells of how each snake carries a pure diamond in its head; again this is of course not true in any way (although some snakes' heads may be covered with a diamond-shaped pattern).

- Quetzalcoatl was a plumed serpent god worshipped by the ancient Aztecs; he was considered the master of all life.

- In some old African cultures, killing a rock python was considered a serious crime, as they worshipped this particular species.

- The vast majority of snakes cannot 'spit' venom – they only inject it with their teeth. However there *are* three species that can spit it up to 3 metres; the venom is aimed at the eyes of their prey and is only used in this way for defence – a blind predator is no longer a threat!

- There have been legends in many cultures of two-headed snakes that possess magical powers. Amazingly, two-headed snakes do exist – this is called Polycephaly, although generally snakes born with this deformity die within a few hours. Of course, they don't possess magical powers, but *are* truly fascinating.

- Some people held a belief that snakes milk cows; this is of course utter rubbish.
- An ancient Australian aboriginal legend tells of a giant rainbow serpent that created all life on earth.
- There is a belief that if you hurt one snake (particularly if it is a tiger snake) then its partner will hunt you down. This is not true in any way – and of course one should never set out to cause harm to a snake anyway!

A Common Adder

Record Breakers

- The longest snake in the world is the *reticulated python*, which can grow up to ten metres in length. There have been reports of examples growing to fifteen metres, but these claims have never been proven.

- It has also been claimed that the largest *anaconda* ever found was almost twelve metres long, but scientists believe this was exaggeration, and 9.5m was the more likely size.

- The anaconda *does* however hold the record for the thickest snake; the biggest one found had a diameter of more than 30cm and thus a circumference of over a metre.

- The *titanboa* is an extinct species which would have regularly reached fifteen metres long; it lived more than sixty million years ago, and so we have only ever found the species' fossilized remains.

- The world's smallest snake is believed to be the *thread snake*, whose fully-grown size is less than four inches long.

- The rarest species of snake is thought to be the *St. Lucia racer*, of which there are less than 100 individuals left.

- The most venomous snake is thought to be the *Belcher's sea snake*; just a couple of milligrams of its venom is strong enough to kill a thousand humans!

- The most venomous snake on land is the *Inland taipan*; just one bite from this species contains enough venom to kill one hundred people.

- An island in Indonesia called Komodo holds the record for having more snakes per square metre of land than any other place on earth.

- The *black mamba* is the fastest-moving snake in the world, reaching speeds of up to 23km/h.

A Black Mamba

Interesting Facts

- A snake can move in four different ways. The first is the *serpentine method*, where the individual pushes off a bump on the surface; this is how most people picture the normal movement of a snake. The second is the *concertina method*, whereby the snake squeezes one portion of its body whilst extending another; this is generally only used in tight spaces. The third method is *sidewinding*, where the snake seems to 'throw' its head forward with the rest of the body following; this is used most often over slippery surfaces such as on desert sand. The final method is *rectilinear*, which is a straight creeping movement.

- Some species of sea snake can take in small amounts of oxygen through their skin, allowing them to dive underwater for longer periods of time.

- Many snakes can see into the infra-red spectrum, using it to their advantage when hunting for prey.

- The black mamba snake's venom contains a pain-relieving compound called *mambalgin*. Scientists are studying this as it is thought this could be used to make a painkiller for humans that is even more effective than morphine.

- There is an island – unsurprisingly called Snake Island – that has been officially quarantined by the Brazilian navy as it has a population of snakes so dense that you are never more than three feet from a dangerous one!

- Up to ten thousand garter snakes can compete to mate with just one single female.

- Whereas humans have around 33 vertebrae, some snakes can have more than four hundred!

- When a snake is swallowing large prey, it can still breathe due to a small tube at the bottom of their mouths which they extend to take in air even when its mouth is full.

- Snakes that are born in eggs have a special tooth (called an 'egg tooth') which is used for ripping their way out when the time is right. This tooth is discarded shortly after hatching.

- Some snakes have small claw-like structures on either side of their *cloaca* (an opening near their tail used for various functions). These are in fact remnants of legs that have reduced considerably in size over millions of years!

An Eastern Milk Snake

The Most Amazing Facts

- If you have ever seen a 'snake charming' performance, you may have wondered what it is about the music that makes the snake sway from side to side. The truth is in fact that it is the *movement* of the instrument used that causes the snake to do this – it would sway even if there was no music playing!

- When a snake eats a large meal, amazingly it can move its heart from where it normally lies to allow the food to move easily through its body!

- A dead rattlesnake can still bite even a few days after it has died – it has heat sensors which remain active until rigor mortis is complete!

- Evolutionary scientists believe that all snakes evolved from a single group of lizards many millions of years ago – amazingly though, we know that they did *not* descend from the legless lizards!

- There is an ancient Chinese belief that if you see a snake in your house it is in fact a good omen, meaning that your family will not starve.

- There are a number of ways one can take a good guess as to whether or not a snake is poisonous. To start with, have a look at the snake's eyes. If the pupils are diamond-shaped then you're likely to be looking at a poisonous species. Colour is another indicator; although not always the case there is even a rhyme which helps: *If red touches yellow it will kill a fellow; red touches black and it's a friend of Jack.*

- Amazingly, some rattlesnakes are learning that their species' rattle alerts humans to their presence and kill them – and are therefore evolving to keep quiet!

- Some male garter snakes pretend to be females so other males 'cuddle up' to them, meaning the 'impressionist' can steal their heat; this is called *kleptothermy*!

- You definitely want to avoid being bitten by the black mamba snake; unfortunately the mortality rate of bites from this species is 95%, so it would mean almost certain death.

- Perhaps the most unusual record involving snakes is that a Malaysian woman kissed a venomous snake fifty-one times in three minutes back in 2006. It should go without saying that this isn't a good idea to try yourself...

A Green Tree Python

And Finally...

- Due to their elastic jaw ligaments, some snakes have been known to eat prey of quite incredible size; a meal consisting of a whole cow is not an unusual feat for some large species. However it has also been observed that *some* snakes actually explode after eating a large meal – and no-one knows why.

A Horned Viper

101 Amazing Facts about Spiders

...and other arachnids

The Basics

- Spiders belong to a group of animals that are called *arachnids*. One defining characteristic of the class is that all arachnids have eight legs.

- Other features of the arachnids include having two distinct body segments, no wings or antennae and an inability to chew.

- As well as spiders, other animals in the arachnid class include scorpions, mites and ticks.

- Spiders are thought to be the most diverse within the arachnid class; it is estimated that there are more than fifty thousand species of them!

- The second most diverse are the mites, with an estimated forty-eight thousand species on the planet.

- Arachnids are part of a group or *phylum* known as the arthropods. Every arthropod has jointed limbs; aside from arachnids, the phylum also includes insects and crustaceans.

- Almost all spiders display predatory activity, and some even eat *other* spiders! The only exception that we know of is one single herbivorous species discovered in 2008 that is named Bagheera kiplingi.

- The first *true* spiders lived around three hundred million years ago, although some spider-like arachnids appeared seventy million years before that.

- Most Spiders have appendages called *spinnerets*. These are organs that produce silk with which the spiders spin webs (although some use the silk to catch their prey in other ways).

- The vast majority of spiders use venom to subdue their prey, injected into a victim through fangs. The only exception we are aware of is the family of spiders called Uloboridae which do not have venom glands.

A Crab Spider

General Facts

- Most spiders have eight eyes, however the number does vary between species. Despite this, a spider's vision is usually nowhere near as strong as its sense of smell.

- Due to the incredible strength of spider silk, scientists are currently studying it in the hope of creating a super-tough material with the same abilities.

- Although it is very rare, there have been instances where clothes have been made out of spider silk. Unlike silk-moths however, farming spiders for their silk is *extremely* difficult and as yet there have not been any economically viable methods found to do this – despite many attempts, including a number that have been patented over the last few hundred years!

- Spiders have short hook-like hairs on their feet which is what allows them to walk on walls and the ceiling.

- Even venomous spiders rarely bite people, and only do so in defence – they have no reason to attack humans!

- You could think of the hairs on a spiders front-most pair of legs as taste organs – spiders often use these to touch their prey and 'taste' it to ensure it is a suitable meal.

- You should consider spiders as welcome guests – they help keep the population of pests such as flies and aphids down.

- On average most spiders live for one or two years, however some tarantulas live for more than twenty!

- Whereas your skeleton is inside your body, a spider's skeleton surrounds it – this is known as an *exoskeleton*.

- Some spiders spin a new web every single day; so as not to waste valuable nutrition, it is not unusual for a spider to eat its own web before starting afresh!

A Tarantula

Other Arachnids

- Mites are amongst the most diverse of all invertebrates, although they generally go unnoticed as they are microscopic in size.

- Despite this, mites are an extremely important part of our ecosystem. Many species are responsible for carrying out decomposition and are found in a range of habitats across the world.

- Some mites on the other hand are problematic to humans; those that colonize human skin can lead to itchy rashes, and many people with hay fever, asthma and eczema find their conditions aggravated by dust mites.

- Ticks are external parasites which usually live on the blood of mammals and birds, but sometimes even on reptiles and amphibians.

- The ticks that live off domestic animals can be particularly problematic, and can devastate herds of livestock in some circumstances.

- There are three families of ticks, although one – the *Nuttalliellidae* – is comprised of a single species, *Nuttalliella namaqua*. The other two families are hard ticks (*Ixodidae*) and soft ticks (*Argasidae*).

- Some arachnids have evolved so that their front two legs have more of a sensory purpose than for walking. In some cases this may even make it difficult to determine that the creature you are looking at has eight legs (as all arachnids do).

- Others have evolved so that extra appendages have grown to the extent that they may look like *additional* legs, giving the appearance that there are *more* than the normal four pairs!

- Another type of arachnid is the order called *Thelyphonida*, also known as whip scorpions (due to their similarity to true scorpions because of their long tails). The largest of these belong to the genus *Mastigoproctus*, whose bodies can reach 8.5cm in length.

- There are further families within the arachnid order, such as tailless whip scorpions (*Amblypygi*), *Opiliones* (which includes harvestmen), *Palpigradi* (very small cousins of whip scorpions) and others.

A Dust Mite

Record Breakers

- The heaviest spider that we know of is the *goliath bird-eating spider*. A captive specimen by the name of Rosi weighed in at 175 grams and had a body length of 119.4mm.

- However, some scientists have challenged this assertion, believing that the *Hercules baboon spider* is in fact heavier. In a recent weigh-off between specimens from the two species at the Natural History Museum, the goliath still came out on top – although as only one example of the Hercules baboon has ever been found (and that was collected from Nigeria over 100 years ago) it may not have been a particularly large one!

- The title of 'largest spider in the world' goes to the *giant huntsman*, due to its enormous leg span. Discovered in a cave in Laos in 2001, it measured a whopping 12 inches across!

- The largest spiders in the USA are also from the huntsman family, although they are sometimes called the *giant crab spider*. Generally found in southern states such as Florida, the very largest can have leg spans of almost 11 inches, although this is *extremely* rare.

- Some species of jumping spider can leap more than 100 times their own body length – that's the same as *you* making the length of two jumbo jets in just one jump!

- The fastest spider in the world (in absolute terms) is the *camel spider*, only found in desert regions. At its fastest it can run across the sand at an amazing twelve miles per hour!

- Relative to its size however, the quickest spider is in fact just a plain old female house spider – it can run over three hundred times its own length in just ten seconds – quicker than a cheetah when taking size into consideration!

- In the UK, the spider with the greatest leg span is the *cardinal spider*, which comes in at up to six inches from front to back leg. It is so named because legend has it that Cardinal Wolsey was terrified of them when he discovered a number of them at the then recently-constructed Hampton court.

- Although it is the subject of some debate, the *Brazilian wandering spider* is generally thought to be the world's most venomous. Also known as the *banana spider*, just 6 micrograms of its venom are enough to kill a mouse – and the spider carries more than 60 micrograms as standard!

- The smallest species of spider is the *patu marplesi*, with adults only reaching 0.43mm in length.

Scorpions

- There are around 1500 species of Scorpion on the planet.

- Scorpions are easily recognisable because of their large front claws, and thin, segmented tail.

- All scorpions have venomous tails, and use these to kill their food and to defend themselves from other predators.

- Around twenty-five species of scorpion are venomous enough to kill a human!

- They are particularly fond of tight spaces where they feel protected – this is my they often hide in people's shoes when they find their way into houses!

- Some female scorpions kill their male partners after they have mated.

- If a mother scorpion is hungry after giving birth, sometimes she just eats her offspring.

- If this doesn't happen however, the baby scorpions will ride around on the mother's back for the first few weeks of their lives.

- Scorpions have between six and twelve eyes – but despite this have very poor vision!

- To make up for this however, they have an excellent sense of smell which allows them to seek out food.

Biology

- The two parts of a spider's body are called the *cephalothorax* and the *abdomen*.

- A spider's eyes, fangs and legs are all found on the cephalothorax, which is the foremost section.

- The spinnerets are found on the abdomen which is the posterior body section.

- The two sections are attached together by what is known as a *pedicel* – you could think of this as the spider's waist.

- The venom glands of a spider are connected to its fangs – or *chelicerae* – by ducts. When biting its prey, the spider's glands contract and push the venom through the ducts and out of the fangs.

- A spider cannot digest solid food and therefore has to turn its prey into liquid before eating it. After paralyzing its victim, the spider covers it with digestive enzymes which break down its tissue.

- Spiders move their legs by a combination of muscles and hydraulics – in fact some of their joints have no muscles at all. To move these, the spider contracts a certain muscle in its body which increases blood pressure thus extending the leg at the joint.

- Jumping spiders use this technique – suddenly increasing the pressure to the relevant joints – to snap their legs out, launching them into the air.

- When mating, the male spider deposits his sperm onto a small bed of silk that he has made which he then stores in a special duct in his body. On finding a female, he will then use his *pedipalps* – appendages near his mouth – to insert the sperm package into her.
- After laying her eggs, a female will protect them with silk, forming an egg sac. Different species produce varying types of egg sac, with some extremely thick for physical protection, whereas others mimic the look of the material on which the eggs are laid for camouflage.

A Black Widow Spider

Unusual Species

- The *ogre-faced spider* catches its prey by weaving a tiny net between its legs and then dangling them around the places they think their prey is likely to pass through.

- The *bolas spider* attaches a spot of sticky glue to the end of a long single line of silk which it swings at moths to catch and eat them.

- The *diving bell spider* creates an air container from its own silk which allows it to spend more than a day underwater, taking in oxygen from the air bubbles it stores in there.

- Of course, *widows* (of various types) are some of the best known examples of dangerous spiders in the world. Although their bites are dangerous to humans if not treated, we have developed fast-acting anti-venoms which are administered if you are unlucky enough to be bitten.

- The *cartwheeling spider* is particularly interesting; living in the Namibian desert, when attacked it will flip onto its side and roll down the sand dunes in its habitat at speeds of up to 44 rpm!

- Perhaps the spider with the most effective camouflage is the *bird dung crab spider*, whose body is covered with blobs and warts that makes it look quite simply like a bird poo. Amazingly, it has even evolved to smell like one as well!

- Beware the various species of *trapdoor spider*, which hide behind a door waiting for prey to wander into their trip lines! Experts in hiding themselves, they are unseen until it is too late!

- The terrifyingly nasty *assassin spider* not only feeds on other spiders, but wears the empty corpses of its victims on its back!

- Maybe the most beautiful looking arachnid, the *peacock spider* has a wonderfully colourful abdomen which it uses to attract females in its courtship ritual.

- Found in parts of Asia, the *myrmarachne plataleoides* is a jumping spider which has evolved to look exactly like a Weaver ant. Most predators avoid weaver ants as they have painful bites, and so the disguise is a very effective one!

A Jumping Spider

Interesting Facts

- Spiders are found on every single continent of the earth except for Antarctica.

- Before a spider exudes silk from its spinnerets, it is actually stored in their bodies in liquid form – it only becomes a solid thread on contact with the air.

- Some species of jumping spider can see ultraviolet light – this is light which is outside of the wavelength range that you and I can perceive.

- Some spiders decorate their webs with extra silk or even other material. It is not known for sure why they do this, however the most popular theory is that it adds extra strength to their constructions.

- The reason that you will often see dead spiders in a 'curled up' position is quite interesting; because they move their legs by hydraulic pressure, if a spider has lost too much water it cannot keep the pressure high enough to stretch out its legs!

- There are a number of tarantulas that cast off certain irritating hairs at predators to deter them from attacking – this can be thought of as similar to a porcupine using its quills for defence.

- Although it is extremely rare these days, there *are* cases where a human has died from a spider bite – although on average this only happens twice a year across the entire planet, so you really shouldn't be scared of it happening to you!

- In the early 1960s, scientists found ways to create anti-venom so that spider bites could be treated – before this happened there were actually significantly more deaths from bites.
- Some spiders rely purely on stealing food from other spiders for their sustenance – and sometimes finish off by killing and eating the spider from who they stole from in the first place!
- All spiders shed their skin – although this happens a great deal more often when they are younger. If you keep a tarantula as a pet, one sign of imminent moulting is the appearance of bald patches, or if it stops eating.

A Golden Orb Spider

Did You Know?

- Most spiders feed on insects and other small invertebrates, however some of the largest species can prey on vertebrates – including mice, lizards and even birds!

- The difference between a *cobweb* and a *spider web* in the English language is that it only becomes a cobweb when the spider abandons it.

- Generally, female spiders of any given species are larger than their male counterparts.

- Although most spiders are solitary creatures, some species live in huge colonies numbering in the thousands; these communal spiders can weave huge intertwined webs in which any prey caught is shared between members.

- Taking into account its weight, spider silk is stronger and tougher than steel.

- Fear of spiders is known as *arachnophobia*; a phobia is technically an *irrational* fear. As humans we really don't have anything to be scared of from spiders, and they deserve our *respect* rather than *fear*.

- Silk is not just used for catching prey – it can be used for shelter, protecting offspring and even reproduction!

- Not all spiders spin webs to catch their prey. Exceptions include wolf spiders and jumping spiders, who each stalk and catch their prey without the aid of a web.

- Spiders often turn up in legend and mythology. One of the most famous is Anansi, the West African trickster god, who is said to bring all stories into the world.

- Another mythological spider tale is the ancient Greek legend of Arachne – in fact where we get the word 'arachnid' from. Arachne was a mortal woman who was so talented at weaving that she challenged Athena, the goddess of crafts and wisdom; as Arachne refused to accept that her skill came from Athena, and so the goddess turned the mortal into a spider so that she and her descendants would have to weave for all time.

A Huntsman Spider

The Most Amazing Facts

- As females are generally larger than males, mating can be quite a risky time for the latter. If a female is hungry, she may decide to eat her prospective partner rather than attempt to reproduce with him!

- Because of this, some spider courtship rituals often involve a display of dancing by the male from a distance – this way he can be fairly sure of his partner's intentions when he approaches her more closely!

- Another interesting courtship ritual is carried out by the *orb spider*. The male of the species will sit on the edge of a female's web and gently pluck a thread, transmitting a very specific vibration to make the female receptive to mating.

- Many people think that the female black widow eats the male after mating, however this is not *always* the case. The *red* widow *does* always do this though – the male willingly sacrifices himself, walking right into the female's mandibles. If she spits him out, he just keeps on walking back in there until she finally enjoys him as a tasty meal!

- Some spiders actually spin decoys of themselves out of silk that 'sit' in the middle of their webs. The idea is that they scare off predators – especially when the decoy is significantly larger than the spider that made it! Amazingly, a few have even been known to shake their webs to make it appear that the decoy is moving – and studies have proven this does in fact work!

- There is a theory which suggests that Little Miss Muffet (of nursery-rhyme fame) was actually based on a real person – her name was Patience, and she was the daughter of Dr Thomas Muffet, a 16th century entomologist who thought that eating spiders could be good for your health!

- Amongst the various experiments conducted on spiders, one unusual one involved giving house spiders different drugs to see how they affected their ability to spin webs. Whereas those constructed when the spiders had been exposed to marijuana, barbiturates and sleeping pills were terrible, the webs built after being exposed to a hallucinogenic drug called LSD were intricately detailed and exceptionally symmetrical – many were even more effective than those spun in 'normal' situations.

- There are some species of spider than have evolved to look like ants. There are two reasons for this – the first is to evade certain predators, whereas the second is to make it easier to prey on the ants that they look like!

- Spiders have been sent into space so we can study how they construct webs – and it seems that they adapt to even the most challenging of conditions. Orb spiders aboard the international space station were able – after a few false starts – to spin strong, symmetrical webs in the zero-gravity environment, and jumping spiders adapted to not being able to leap onto their prey by sidling along their web and stretching out to catch their victims.

► Compared to their size and weight, spiders are surprisingly intelligent. This is down to their comparative brain size. Amazingly, some spiders have brains that are so large their other organs actually overflow into their legs!

A Tiger Spider

And Finally...

- There is a dance called the *tarantella* which originated in Italy in the 16th century. At the time, it was thought that if you were bitten by a certain species of wolf spider, you would die if you did not engage in frenzied dancing. The species of spider was called the *tarantula*, although this word has now come to describe a completely different family of spiders!

A Goliath Bird Eating Spider

101 Amazing Facts about Fish

General Facts – Part 1

- A fish's fins are used for balance, propulsion and communication.

- Most fish have excellent eyesight. They are especially good at seeing colours and choosing the best spot for camouflage.

- A number of fish together are called a *school*. Sometimes schools contain millions of individuals.

- Fish don't sleep in the same way as humans. Although they slow down and their metabolic rate reduces, their brainwaves to not change in the same way that other animals' do.

- Some fish don't have 'normal' teeth but a kind of grinder in their throats to help prepare what they swallow for digestion. These are called *pharyngeal* teeth.

- Most fish can't swim backwards for anything more than a few inches.

- Not all fish have scales – sharks, for instance, have skin which is rough and textured like sandpaper.

- Scientists are discovering new species of fish all the time; at the last count there were around 35,000 species recorded.

- Fish are cold-blooded; this means that their internal body temperature changes in response to the temperature of their environment.
- Fish were well established on earth long before the dinosaurs came along.

A school of sardines

Unusual Fish – Part 1

- The *fangtooth* is a scary looking fish. Although the entire fish is only a few inches long, its two large fans are around an inch long themselves and when its mouth is closed they rest in sockets to the side of its brain!

- The *archerfish* is so named because it can shoot a stream of water much like an arrow at insects perched on branches dangling above the water.

- The *European catfish* has an unusual method of finding a meal. It will swim right up to the shore, purposefully luring pigeons close to it, making them think they are in for a tasty fish treat. However it then turns the tables on the birds by lunging at one and dragging it into the water for its dinner!

- The *ocean sunfish* is the heaviest known bony fish in the world, doesn't have a tail and lays 300 million eggs every year.

- *Arowanas* are freshwater fish which can jump out of the water to catch prey such as small birds and bats!

- The male of the *Banggai cardinalfish* species keeps eggs safe in its mouth until they are ready to hatch.

- The *electric eel* can discharge enough electricity to kill a horse. Only the front 20% of the eel contains vital organs; the rest of it contains the organs which produce the electricity!

- The male *emperor angelfish* has a small harem of females – up to five follow him around wherever he goes. If he dies, then one of the females turns into a male and becomes the new leader.

- The *sand tiger shark* can adjust its buoyancy by burping at the surface; this means that it can effectively 'hover' motionless in the water.

- The *hammerhead shark* swims in schools of over 500 individuals; at the centre of the school is the strongest female. When it is time to mate, she shakes her head from side to side which acts as a signal for the other female sharks to move away – thus ensuring she becomes the centre of attention from the males!

An ocean sunfish

Seahorses

- Seahorses are the only fish that regularly swim upright.
- They are also the only fish with necks!
- The seahorse can move each of its eyes separately to see as much of its surroundings as possible – it can even have one eye looking forwards whilst the other looks backwards!
- Like a chameleon, the seahorse can change its colour to blend in with its surroundings.
- Adult seahorses mate for life.
- Some seahorses swim in pairs with their tales linked together!
- Seahorses are different to most other creatures in the animal kingdom – the female lays her eggs inside a pouch on the male's chest, and it is he who incubates them until they are ready to hatch. This means they are one of the few species of animal we know of where the male gives birth to the young.
- We have so far discovered 53 species of seahorse ranging from two to thirty centimetres long. Seahorses are found across the world, from coral reefs to mangrove forests.
- Seahorses need to eat constantly as they do not have stomachs!
- The courtship dance of some seahorses lasts eight hours, is intricately choreographed and involves energetic movements and colour changes.

A seahorse in a coral habitat

Did You Know?

- The catfish has four times the number of tastebuds that you do.

- Fish are far from silent creatures. They talk to each other through grunts, croaks, whistles, hisses, clacking of teeth and much more! Although they have no vocal chords they use various parts of their bodies to make these noises.

- A fish's jaw is not connected to its skull – this means that some species can quickly extend their mouths to grab prey which wrongly thinks it is far enough away!

- Most fish have tastebuds all over their body, not just in their mouths!

- A fish's tail can tell you a lot about the nature of the fish. If the tail is 'split', the fish is a fast one and may cover huge distances. If the tail is not split (and is usually quite large), the fish probably lives near to a coral reef or similar habitat.

- Clownfish and sea anemones have a symbiotic relationship; as it is poisonous to other fish except the clown, the anemone protects it from predators. The clownfish also defends the anemone from potential predators as well as cleaning it from parasites.

- When should you use the word fish and when should you say fishes? The former is used when referring to a single species (i.e. eight trout are eight fish), whereas the latter is for multiple species... for instance six trout and four salmon would be ten fishes!

- Someone who studies fish is called an *ichthyologist*.
- Neither starfish nor jellyfish are actually fish!
- A fish's centre of gravity is generally high up on its body. This is why when a fish dies it normally turns over, as the heaviest part will sink lowest without the waving of the find to keep balance.

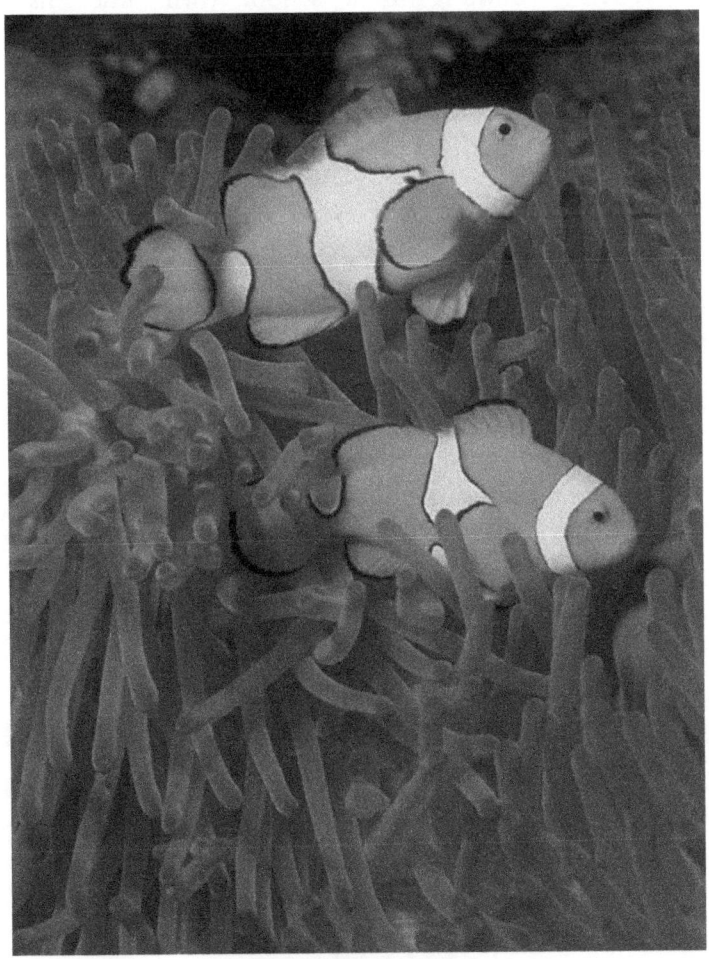

Clownfish living with an anemone

Amazing Facts

- Fish are used in the manufacture of many surprising products across the world. For instance, did you know that almost all lipstick for sale today contains fish scales?!

- When swimming in a school with other fish, individuals keep their place not only by looking around them but also by sensing movement of their 'neighbours' with a row of pores along their sides called a lateral line.

- Fish do not add new scales as the grow – their existing scales just get larger!

- The puffer fish is a delicacy in japan where it is known as *Fugu*. However, one has to be *extremely* careful preparing it because it also contains deadly toxin! To ensure Japanese gourmets aren't regularly poisoned, chefs who wish to prepare Fugu must attend a special course and prove they can serve it safely.

- There is a genus of fish called the *anableps*. These amazing creatures have four eyes – two above the water and two below!

- Fish do actually have noses, although they play no part in respiration as they do in humans. A fish's nose is used for smelling prey and for navigation.

- During Roman times, a fish called the *Salema porgy* was taken as a recreational drug! Eating one gives you auditory and visual hallucinations that last more than a day.

- There are more species of fish in the Amazon river alone than can be found in the whole of Europe.
- Some experts believe that over the past 100 years, 80% of the biomass of fish in the world's oceans has been lost (well, mostly consumed...) due to commercial fishing.
- Well-known American writer Ernest Hemingway was also a keen fisherman. He developed a number of new techniques to improve his catch rate when fishing in the sea. Although some were quite innovative and enabled him to catch seven marlin in just one day – a world record at the time – others were not particularly sporting... such as shooting sharks with a sub-machine gun.

A great white shark

General Facts – Part 2

- Most fish reproduce with the female laying eggs and the male fertilising them.

- Newly hatched fish are called 'fry'.

- Great white sharks are one exception to this rule however – they actually give birth to live young, which are known as pups.

- It is common for fish to change sex (both from male to female and from female to male) as part of their reproductive process.

- Relative to their body size, fish actually have quite small brains compared to other animals.

- Fish are divided into three main groups: *cartilaginous* (whose body-frames are cartilage not bone), *bony* and *lobe-finned* (such as lungfish and coelacanths).

- The oldest known goldfish ever was called Goldie and lived to be 45 years old!

- The whale shark lays the largest eggs of any animal; in the 1950s one was found that was more than 35cm long!

- The first public aquarium was opened in London in 1853.

- fish are the most popular pets today in the United States, with around 12 million households owning aquariums.

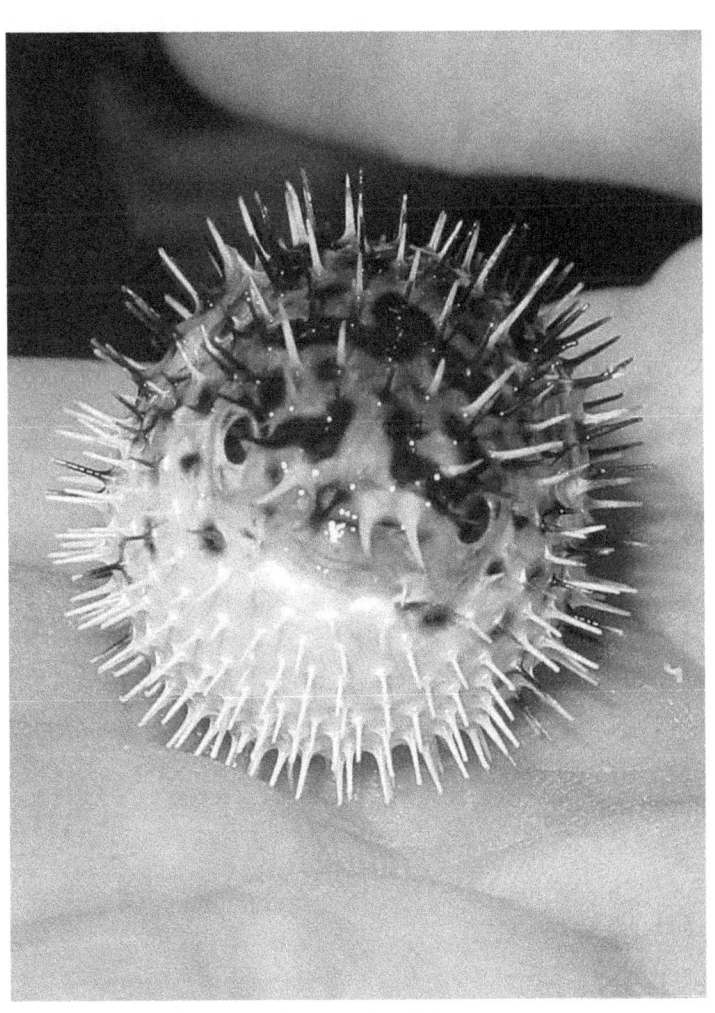

A porcupine fish

Unusual Fish – Part 2

- The *male anglerfish* is miniscule in comparison to the female. Whilst the male is around four centimetres in length, the female is fifteen times as long! The species mates for life... although the female achieves this by absorbing the male into her body!

- When *salmon* are born, they usually spend their early life in rivers, and as they are maturing they swim out to see. Here they gain significant body mass and become fully-fledged adults. When they are ready to have young of their own, they amazingly find their way back to where they were born, often jumping up waterfalls and over natural obstructions. Here they spawn, and then die, completing the circle of life.

- The *mudskipper* can survive out of water for enormous amounts of time – in fact it lives on land more than it does underwater! It carries water inside its gill chambers and can even breathe through its skin!

- The *lungfish* is even more amazing – it can live out of water for years! It can bury itself underground inside a slimy cocoon it has made, and breathes air through a tube the pokes out at the surface.

- During their larval development stage, one of the eyes of *flounders* and *soles* actually migrates to the other side of their head! This allows them to bury themselves in the sand with both eyes facing upwards so they can ambush prey that happens to swim above them.

- The *stone fish* is the most poisonous fish in the world; if you step on one it will almost certainly paralyse you, and if you're not treated immediately you will most likely die. Scary!

- The famous *piranha fish* has razor-sharp teeth which allow it to eat animals much bigger than itself. A group of piranhas can even attack, kill and eat a horse if it happens to be wading across their habitat. The word piranha comes from the Brazilian words *pira nya* which means scissors. Despite their fearsome reputation however, there has *never* been a reported case of piranhas attacking and killing a human!

- The *batfish* has a cunning way of dealing with danger – it lies on its side motionless, making predators assume it is just a dead leaf passing by.

- The *black swallower fish* can eat prey that is ten times heavier and twice as long as itself! They swallow their opponents whole, storing them in a huge sac underneath their body which slowly digests whatever is inside.

- The *porcupine fish* can make itself large to scare off predators. It swallows water which it stores in its stomach making it like a great big round ball – amazingly it can reach a diameter of almost one metre!

Sharks

- Sharks are the only fish which have eyelids.

- Almost a quarter of a great white shark's entire bodyweight is made up just from its huge liver.

- Before it is born, when a sand tiger shark pup has consumed all of the yolk within its own egg sac, it proceeds to eat the other eggs – and embryos – in its mother's womb! Despite this, the female will give birth to two pups. How? She has two wombs!

- The shark cage was invented by Rodney Fox after he was attacked by a great white. He only just survived, nearly bleeding to death and requiring 462 stitches.

- Elephants kill fifty times as many people every year as sharks do. In fact, even deer kill ten times an many!

- Because sharks do not have a swim bladder helping to keep them afloat, if they stop swimming they sink to the bottom of the sea.

- The gestation period of a shark can be anything up to two years!

- Only 20 of the 400 or so species of sharks have ever been known to attack humans.

- Sharks have between five and fifteen rows of teeth in each jaw. A single tooth usually falls out after just one week, however a 'conveyer belt' like system shifts the next one into place!

▶ Humans are a huge threat to sharks. It is thought that seventy million are killed every year just for their fins which are used in some countries for cooking – despite the fact that shark fin has no taste of its own.

A whitetip reef shark

Record Breakers

- It is thought that the oldest ever fish was a *Koi* by the name of Hanako. She was born in 1751 and didn't die until 1977, making her an amazing 226 years old! Her age was confirmed by scientists who analysed her scales under a microscope.

- Although it doesn't fly (rather it actually glides through the air), the *flying fish* regularly soars distances of 200 metres and can reach over a metre above the water's surface. The longest glide ever observed was an incredible 400 metres!

- The largest fish we know of is the *whale shark*; the biggest specimen recorded was 12.65m long and weighed 21.5 tons. Sailors, divers and marine biologists however often report seeing even bigger examples, some around 15m long!

- The *sailfish* is believed to be the fastest in the world; it has been measured swimming at speeds of up to 68 miles per hour!

- The slowest fish in the world is thought to be the *dwarf seahorse* which takes one hour to move just five feet!

- The most primitive fish we are still aware of today are *lampreys* and *hagfish*; the latter are the only known animals to have a skull but no vertebrae and also hold the record for the world's slimiest creature – one single hagfish can produce an entire bucket of slime in just one minute!

- We think that the smallest fish in the world is the *Paedocypris progenetica* from Indonesia; adult females of this species only reach 7.9mm in length.

- The world's oldest fishhook was found in 2011 in East Timor. It was 42,000 years old.

- It is thought that the myth of the sea serpent is actually based on a real-life fish. The *Oarfish* is the longest bony fish, growing to an incredible 56 feet in length – that's around 17 metres!

- In 2013 at Tokyo's Tsukiji market, someone paid the equivalent of 1.8 million US dollars for a 222-kilogram Bluefin tuna, making it the single most expensive fish ever sold!

A flying fish

The Most Amazing Facts

- During lent, the only meat that the Catholic church allows its followers to eat is salted fish. However, because people got very bored of fish at every supper for forty days, the church actually changed the definition of 'fish' to include puffins, beavers and turtles, as they can all swim.

- Some farmers keep goldfish in cattle troughs as they keep the water clean by eating algae. Amazingly, the goldfish do pretty well in such an unusual environment!

- The flesh from farmed salmon has to be artificially dyed pink, as they don't have the same diet of krill and shrimp that their counterparts in the wild do.

- Using selective breeding processes, Japanese scientists created goldfish with see-through skin. You can actually see their hearts beating!

- Despite the myth that goldfish have extremely short memories, they can actually recognise their owners and even beg for food once they have learned who normally feeds them!

- Apparently, there are laws in both Ohio and Oklahoma stating that it is illegal to get a fish drunk!

- In Japan there is a chain of restaurants called *Zauo* in which your table is a boat floating on the surface of an aquarium. You catch your own fish which is cooked for you by a chef!

- A highly social fish called the *mosquitofish* has proven in experiments that it can count to 100! They learned to count the number of objects painted on doors which they had to choose to swim through to meet back up with the rest of their school!

- If you catch a *sturgeon* in the United Kingdom, by law you have to give it to the queen (or king) as it is known as a 'royal fish'.

- The *bristlemouth* is the world's most common fish, however you're unlikely to ever see one as they live deep down in the ocean and have extremely good camouflage.

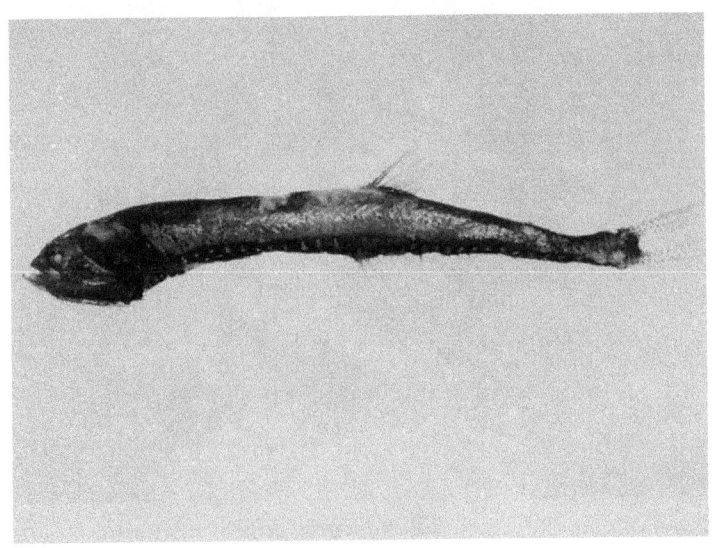

A bristlemouth

And Finally...

- We have only explored around 1% of the oceans in the world. It is thought there are likely to be millions of species of which we are currently unaware.

An adult emperor angelfish

Also from Jack Goldstein

www.ingramcontent.com/pod-product-compliance
Lightning Source LLC
Chambersburg PA
CBHW032105090426
42743CB00007B/242